* SIX FEET APART *
ANTHOLOGY

_____

THE WRITERS GROUP

SIX FEET APART

ISBN# 9798465247139

Edited By :
Matthew Davenport { Corvus Copy & Media }

Cover Design By:
Kora Sadler

Other Books By The Writers Group
Internal Voice Carved In Black
Many Shades Of Voices
Now With Page Numbers
The Forthcoming
Take Five
Six Feet Apart

Dedication

This book is dedicated to the wonderful people that made it possible. Many thanks to all the Aspiring Authors who motivate us to come   together and write.

A Very Special Thanks To:

The Writers Group Members & Sponsors

Akron-Summit County Public Library / Kenmore Branch

Jennifer Meredith & Event Team @ Barnes & Noble Fairlawn

Mike Matonis @ DriveTV USA

Dr. Joanne Dowdy

Steven Pryce

Rui Xu

Hollie Petit

What Will Carol Do Next! Event Planning Services

Russell and Angelica Henley

The Write Stuff Authors Group of Canton

Cleveland Writers Group

Everyone @ Meetup.com

Hope Bolinger

Joshua Lisec

William A. Gordon

Bre Stephens

Table of Contents

A Letter Home for Dad

by Joanne Kilgour Dowdy

Dear Dad,

This is your day! I can't help but think about you as the morning arrives. Your words of advice echo in my ear as I review the events that took place at the last house that I rented. The cat and mouse game with Mr. Kay finally came to a head just as you would have predicted. After all those complaints that I made about the repairs that needed to be done, the straw that the camel needed arrived in the flooding of the kitchen sink. Can you believe that Mr. Kay arrived at the house with a plunger! He was going to fix the kitchen sink all by himself. I looked him in the eye and told him that I was not letting him in the house. He had to send a plumber to fix the problem, I explained. Then, I walked off and left him in the driveway. This was the showdown that was three years in the making.

Dad, imagine me standing inside the front door at the house that I have rented for four years. I told you before that this neighborhood is considered upscale and many people are not happy that my home is a rental. I have heard from neighbors that some people would rather that the place be remodeled and sold to a family that is more like the well-to-do neighbors who have lived on this block for many years.

Well, this is what took place in full view of my neighbors one day. My landlord, Mr. Kay, was standing just outside the front door below the third step. He told me that he came to deliver a notice that he was going to sell the house. It is now official, I say to myself, that he will change the lease from an annual contract to a monthly rental. I ask him to come into the house, rather than continue standing in the cold outside the door. Since I am always careful not to get too cold and get sick, I wanted the door to be closed behind us and the meeting to take place inside the house. Who needs the neighbors to witness the whole drama on the front steps? Mr. Kay looked wary. Maybe he never intended to speak with me. He may have planned to leave the letter in my mailbox or just slip it under the door so that he would not have to deal with me when he brought the news. His anxiety is a result of the fact that I refused to let him into the house with the plunger when the kitchen sink flooded.

When Mr. Kay stepped inside the door, his eyes looked up to the shelves that are to the left of the entrance. He noticed that those shelves were empty. Beside the shelving unit was a stack of boxes that obviously were full. They were stacked away from the wall where the shelves and cupboards were once full of pictures. Maybe he was thinking that I had already found a place to live and that it did not matter that he was changing the lease from an annual to a monthly contract.

Because I had talked to a friend about the situation with Mr. Kay, I already knew that my landlord could change his rental policy and force me to move out sooner than his first lease had allowed. My annual contract had expired so I was, in fact, on the renewed agreement for the next year.

I did not mind moving out of the house, but I very much felt offended that Mr. Kay did not care to take care of problems when I requested that he make repairs to the house. What was I thinking when I noticed the number of ways in which it was obvious that Kay was not going to do right by his tenant? For instance, he dragged his feet to repair the pipes in the bathroom.

This was a follow-up act from the first week when I moved in and he acted like he did not know that the basement floor was always damp, and therefore, he should not have put down giant rugs over the floor. I pointed out to him that the rugs would smell bad eventually, so he removed them from the basement. The boxes with my belongings had soaked up two inches of water by that time.

When I showed him the windows that were painted shut, he made no effort to unseal them. On another day, I explained that one room had a damaged vent that did not allow heat or air conditioning to service the space. This last fact was never mentioned until I complained for the third year that I had no heat in my bedroom. His "friend" who came to check out the heating system explained that the unit was not attached to the vent leading into the bedroom. Nothing could be done to direct air to that space.

Mr. Kay's last-ditch attempt to rid himself of me and my requests for repairs, including the fact that I was planning to report him to the court that handled rental issues, was the final paragraph in a long, boring story. It was more old than boring, honestly. The last week of my four-year stay under Kay's management led me to write in my journal: "What occurred to me as I was packing up to leave this three-bedroom house on a quiet tree-lined street near a lake that was considered a historical treasure, was the fact that I never forgot that it was on loan.

Every month, from the first of forty-eight, I had to call the landlord to fix the drain or other parts of the house that needed attention. He always came to look at the problem, eventually deciding if he should have a go at the repairs himself or call in a professional to repair the damage. Replacing things in disrepair was never on the menu of options for Mr. Kay."

Before he came to the house though, he gave me the "FBI" treatment. This is what I called his questioning style about the most recent complaint. Mostly, he would begin his series of questions—the interrogation as I came to think of it —with the question "What did you do?" Many months after I became accustomed to this treatment, I told him that he was doing an "FBI" question style, and I pointed out that I wouldn't call him to do repairs if I didn't think that the house needed his serious attention. I believe that my experience supported my understanding that "Living in a racist environment is like renting a house from a slumlord."

I concluded my entry in the journal one day: "As long as this country supports people who think that Euro-Americans, and people who look like their descendants, are the only heirs to the benefits that this democracy represents, we will always have people who suffer under the hardships that slumlords represent.

Even if we can get people into "safe" housing, where they are supposed to breathe clean air and enjoy the healthy environment afforded by a high tax rate and very committed public servants in various government positions, we will all be the silent neighbors who watch the abuse of power work its effects on those who do not have the knowledge or capacity to defend themselves against such tyranny. It is in everyone's best interest to speak up when we know that power is being misappropriated. If not, neighborhoods and other spaces where communities are supposed to thrive will be undermined to the disadvantage of the whole country."

Dad, this entry was made in my daily journal two years before Americans stormed the Capitol in Washington on January 6, 2021. Two years before the riots across the country demonstrated the level of frustration that Americans of every racial, social, and economic class walked in the streets following the murder of George Floyd by a white police officer. I was not delusional in my understanding that being black, female, and an immigrant did not work in my favor in this upscale white neighborhood near the university campus. To say that I was out of place in this neighborhood would be an understatement if one was to do a cursory glance around at the people who lived in the houses on the blocks surrounding the rental property. But Dad, across from my home was the residence of a colleague who formerly taught at the same university where I was employed. We enjoyed the same economic status. I had more credentials than he had as far as university degrees, and my career had taken me to live and work in several states in this country. This colleague had lived in two states his entire life. He was retired and I was two years away from retirement when I moved away from his neighborhood. We enjoy each other's company and I have become a family friend who feels and is embraced, as an important part of my neighbor's social network.

Maybe it was my attitude about the journey in my career that was influencing my interactions with Mr. Kay. Do you think? Four years is a long time to put up with someone's blatant disregard about their responsibilities as a landlord. I was worn down by this shabby treatment and realized that my health was impaired because the house was not being maintained properly. After calling in a professional company to test the air quality, I found out that the air was polluted by an unclean heating and air conditioning unit. The unit had not been cleaned in 12 years. I was breathing dirty air for four years! Whether or not I felt physically ready or willing to find a new place to live, my subconscious was telling me that it was time to move on. My health status was screaming for relief from the environment.

This was the year that I had hopes of retiring or resigning. It just seemed that I had done everything that was possible to keep myself productive and engaged with the students since I began teaching in 2001. My ability to publish and not perish remained consistent since 2009, when I was promoted to full professor.

I was proud to wear the mantle of being the first black woman to make full professor in the College of Education in its first 100 years. It was true that my role as a leader in research and publication was important to the college. I knew about my being a role model for the few non-white faculty and students who were members of our academic community. We all know when we have done our "bit" and need to move on.

My friend, Cindy, told me that 2018 was a "golden year" for me. She is a clairvoyant and has given me interesting insights about my journey over the last fifteen

years. It helped me to keep doing my job. I cannot thank Cindy enough for her encouragement over the years. You would like Cindy, Dad. She works with found objects and creates spectacular masks for art collectors. She likes to sell work by other artists in her store and displays all kinds of crystals and precious stones in her gallery. When I think about Cindy's "reading" of astrological signs for 2018, however, it seems strange that the year when I was moving my home under very stressful circumstances and the time period when I was so very sick that I could not teach for a whole semester, could be called a "golden year." What I understand now, since hindsight is always perfect, is that the time I took to regroup in a new home and convalesce from an "angry pancreas" was the window of opportunity that afforded me enough space to set new goals for my career and lifestyle.

You won't believe this, but I'm going to tell you anyway. A month after I moved out of the house with the bad plumbing and dirty air system, I was driving along the main road that ran outside the old neighborhood on my way home from an errand. As I approached the entrance to the cemetery in that town, I began to vomit all over myself, and it spilled onto the steering wheel. The feeling to throw up came out of nowhere. I was not sick the minute before I saw a plume of liquid coming out of my mouth and spreading over my clothes, pooling in my lap, and spraying the dashboard. I kept driving as I reached out to my right to find something to stop the flow of liquid coming from me. The bile smelled like my breakfast. I reached out the passenger seat and grabbed a plastic bag that was sitting there. Putting this bag to my mouth, I then turned the car into the entrance of the cemetery that was on my right. I wanted to get out of

the lane with traffic quickly to avoid any accidents if I suddenly stopped. I planned to park the car inside the cemetery so I could clean up the mess that was dripping on me from my mouth and about to fall through my dress onto the floor of the car.

As I was turning into the cemetery, a driver in the car on my left side looked over to me and seemed to register shock at what he saw. This man witnessed my gushing mouth as I scrambled to contain it even as I steered the car in the right lane. He did not stop or come back to assist me. His car was in the left lane, and it had to keep moving or there was going to be a serious accident. Maybe the driver doubted what he saw in my car and the strange scene compelled him to keep the car moving in the traffic. Or, he may have thought that I was drunk—maybe even hungover—or recovering from a long night of drinking. I was in serious pain, regardless of what it looked like to the world around me, and I needed to get to the nearest medical facility to find out what was going on inside of my stomach. My first decision was to get home and change my clothes. Can you believe that? Since this life-changing event took place on a Saturday, I knew that I could get to the nearest Express Clinic in my town that very day.

However, I decided on the way home that my stomach was upset from eating some seafood the previous night. I convinced myself that I could take a cold shower, lay down for the rest of the day, and the sick feeling would pass. In my mind, I was convinced that I would be normal the next day. That was a bad idea and it led to a worse outcome since the pain in my stomach continued all day and all night.

I could not get any rest. When the sun came up on Sunday morning, I took myself to the emergency room ten minutes from my house. At that point Dad, I could barely stand up straight. This visit to the emergency room was the beginning of a hospital stay that lasted five days. I was checked in, the doctor decided to do a scan to see what was going on in my stomach, and then I was sent to the hospital in an ambulance. This was the first time in my life that I had this experience as a patient. An ambulance, Dad! It occurred to me on the way to the hospital that no one knew where I was. When I left the house, all I had with me was my wallet. I don't keep a phone with me all the time.

Between the pain racking my body and my anxiety about what could be wrong with me, I just wanted to get out of the house and drive to the emergency room as fast as I could after getting dressed. I had no idea when I left the house that I would be gone from my home for a week. My car remained in the parking lot outside the emergency building for several days. The same day that I arrived in the hospital, I was told that I had acute pancreatitis and the only thing that the doctors could do was wait until it calmed down. The first doctor who attended to me explained that they would keep me hydrated and continue checking the pancreas to see what was developing as the days proceeded. The bad news, or the worse news that day, was that I would not be able to eat anything for the time that my pancreas was in distress.

Of course, the doctor informed me, they would do blood work every day and I would have to stay in bed until they felt that they could release me to go home and check in with my own doctor. Dad, believe it when I say that a part of me was rejoicing that I would lose weight because of this illness. I was looking hard for the bright side of the darkest time.

I have never been sick like that in my life. Do you have any recollection of taking me to a hospital? Ever? Was I ever in need of help with a broken leg or arm? Never! I hope that I will never be sick like that time in 2018 ever again. Not only was I in physical pain, but I kept wondering if my mental distress about the circumstances under which I had to move out from the old rental was a significant part of this dilemma. Since I was hospitalized just before the start of the school semester, it meant that I would have to miss the first week of school. It was traditional to have department meetings during the first official week of duty back on campus. I did not feel very sad about missing those days. I was more concerned about being absent for the first classes with my students when I would begin learning their names and personalities. It would be hard to get into the groove of teaching the three groups of pre-service teachers if I did not have the important "first impressions" that helped to solidify the impact of each group's personality on me.

Since I live alone, I always think of certain colleagues as the first people to call on if I get into any hassles off the campus. It made sense that it was my director who was the first person that I called to tell about my stay in the hospital. Dr. Alex turned up one day when I was taken to another floor in the hospital to get a scan. It was unfortunate that she could not greet me, but she left a novel thinking that it would help me pass the time in bed. The second person that I contacted was my hairdresser who had known me for thirteen years at that point. Mimi and I once made plans for her to help me when I had another medical procedure done

at the hospital. We knew that I would need to stay in bed until I fully recuperated. It was important, she told me, that I made arrangements for someone to bring me food and assist me when I needed to change clothes and move around the house.

Not in our wildest imaginations, Dad, did Mimi and I ever think that I would end up in hospital a year before our plans were put in action. Mimi answered her phone in church, which happened to be near the hospital, and promised to come right over as soon as the service was done. She soon arrived at the hospital, ready to do whatever was necessary to get me comfortable and more accepting of my unhealthy condition. To her credit, she never showed any panic and proceeded to turn up every day that I was in that hospital bed. She was going through the final stages of her divorce proceedings, but she still managed to check on me that week. I asked her to move the car from the parking lot outside the emergency room and go to the house to water my plants. You taught me to show appreciation for every blessing that is given to my life, and I am eternally grateful to Mimi for her camaraderie and loyalty under stressful circumstances.

Mimi also promised to get me some food that I would be interested in eating, since the hospital fare would leave me feeling more unhappy than the pain in my side. For all the days that I was in bed in that room, my side felt like I was on fire every time I moved any part of my body.

Dad, have you ever had a long stay in a hospital? What about taking a ride in one of the beds that they kept you in while you were healing? I had a lot of fluid in me, my doctor explained, and they needed a clear picture of my abdomen to

see what was happening on the inside. Taking a ride on that bed that I seemed to be married to, through the halls of the ward and moving in and out of the elevator, left me feeling that I was on serious hallucinogens. When we got to the room where the image was taken in a dark setting, it felt like I had been shot from the belly of an airplane into the sky. It was so dark in that room. The cold was mind-numbing, too. Where was I? What was happening? Who was the man telling me how to breathe while he made clicking sounds with machines from another room? I was glad to get back to my hospital room and relax in a now familiar space. It was great that I did not have to hold my breath because I was afraid that I might tip out of the bed on the journey to the x-ray room. The thought of having to move any limb as I tried to get back in the position that was least uncomfortable seemed like it would be cruel and unusual punishment.

What I liked about my director, Dr. Alex, was that she was kind enough to leave her office in the next town and come visit me while I was down and out. She did not know that the pain I was enduring left me so weak that I could not concentrate on reading anything, including the list of phone numbers posted on the wall in front of me.

When people called on my phone in the room, after I had left messages for them to call me at the hospital, I was unable to focus my eyes on the printed numbers on the poster in front of the bed. I would tell friends and colleagues to call the hospital and ask for me by room number if they needed to contact me. It was not my intention to be a difficult patient; the fact was that I was weak from pain and hunger and saving my energy to crawl out of bed, dragging the bag of fluid on the carrier along with me, and get to the bathroom safely. The return journey to the bed was even more demanding because I had to climb up to the level of the mattress and heave myself onto the bed so that I could then turn around to face the ceiling and get settled in the middle of the sheets. The next big effort involved getting the spread from under me and covering my body with the sheet and two blankets that I needed to keep me warm while I lay like a beached whale most of the day.

As the days passed, the telephone operator for the hospital who was on duty most times that I made calls became familiar with my voice. She was kind and helped me get through to my office and the friends who needed to know where I was. Her patience ran out, however, when I asked her to place a long-distance call to Florida. This dear woman kindly reminded me that I was being given a courtesy call each time that she answered my request. I explained that I was in the hospital, in bed, and in need of letting people know where I was. My compromise with her was that I would call my office and ask one of the assistants there to call the people who needed to know that I was in the hospital and had to cancel appointments with them.

It slipped me, in my painful condition, to explain that I was in the hospital with my wallet and the clothes that the ambulance brought me in. Nothing more. It would have made my case even more desperate if I explained to her that I did not plan to stay at the hospital for five days when I left my home on Sunday morning. If I had made this clear, I now believe, she might have had more sympathy for me. Who knows? By the last day of my stay in the hospital, however, I was at ease with the routine of making calls, and everyone who had to find me could do so by calling me on the phone in my room.

Dr. Fitz, my doctor, decided that I was on the road to mending and wanted to send me home on the Friday of my week in the hospital. Would you call that good luck? I was afraid to go home to an empty house and told my doctor that I would be better off staying in the hospital a little longer. He, dear soul, was concerned that I would be exposed to catching germs and believed that it was better for me to recuperate in my own surroundings. He was so worried about me refusing to leave his care that he found a counselor to come in and talk to me about hiring a home assistant for when I left the hospital. Fortunately, one of my former students called me at the hospital after reaching out to several people who he thought would help him get a message to me. He was shocked to find out that I was answering a phone in the hospital. It made him very upset that he tried to reach me at home and because I did not answer his call, he began to worry about my whereabouts. Dr. Zyang then told me that he was going to come to Ohio, from California, and check on me. This news lifted my spirits, and when I delivered my decision to leave the hospital to the doctor, he was equally relieved that I was going home. I suppose he was glad to get rid of his "favorite problem" for that week. Mimi brought him flowers when she returned to my room after one of her runs to do errands.

I started feeling better as I thought of Dr. Zyang visiting me at the house to help as I recovered from my less angry pancreas.

My recuperation took up all three months of the semester. It was the first time that I was sick and missed school for such a long stint. That is seventeen years on the job without taking sick leave, Dad. Were you that good about going to work? Even when you were training for the Olympics in Helsinki? Seventeen years is a long time to find your way to a well-deserved break from a grueling routine on your job, right? As I began to heal, I found that my mind spent a lot of time considering what it would be like to stop teaching every year and find other ways to use my hard-won freedom. What would I do if I no longer had to race out of bed on the coldest days of the year, get dressed, drive to work, and start my day in a classroom or a meeting with colleagues? How would I order my time to make me feel useful and fulfilled at the end of each day?

Given the space to explore my life away from the drama and high energy demands of life on the campus, I had ample time to read what I wanted, plan my exercise time, get in touch with friends and family on my own schedule, and adopt good eating habits. I know you never had such leisure in your life. You must be thinking that I am the acme of living like a princess. It's not all that it seems, Dad. Believe me, all that glitters is not gold, as you often told me when I was growing up. What weighed on me every day of my time on sick leave was the three medical procedures that were required to get me back in good working order. I was also forced to slow down and think deeply about what it meant to be "successful" and to have a caring community around me.

Over the course of the three months that I was at home recovering from my bout with acute pancreatitis, I had the privilege of being visited by at least eighteen friends, students, and colleagues. This was an eye-opening experience and heart-warming, Dad. Before those days at home, I could never guess that there was such a large group of people who would take time out of their day to call or visit

me when I went missing from my duties at the college. Yes, indeed, I was surprised to find students who were in class with me at least a year before this semester had turned up at my door. Word of mouth travels fast among a social network like ours at school, and people find out what is going on without even trying to be in anyone's business. True talk, no lie. I had offers of food and caring notes sent by email often. Three colleagues who had worked on projects with me turned up to drive me to the hospital when I needed my procedures and then waited two or three hours to bring me home.

Other associates took me to doctors' appointments and sat in the room with me when the doctor explained my condition and the steps that needed to be taken so that I could become healthy. People reminded me that I could call them at any time of day or night, and they would turn up to help me. It was a great comfort to know that there was a loving community supporting and assuring me that I did not need to feel abandoned because I was not on the campus every day. That fact was due to half my recovery.

This experience of coming to understand that I had a place in this town with people who had known me from the day that I began teaching at the college was a great part of the reasoning that led me to consider staying put in town after I retired in 2020.

Up until that shocking news about me needing to go to the hospital, and then staying there for five days, I had no plans to stay near the campus very long after my final semester teaching. My friends, students, and colleagues helped me to understand that I would have to start from scratch in any town that I decided to move to once my

teaching career was over. The hard work that I had done to establish ties with people who worked with me, or did any outings for recreation, was the basis of my bond with each of them. I would have to begin building relationships in a new town with different people if I decided to give up the known for the unknown in my life.

And, Dad, what about that "nuisance factor"—the impact of racism on all interactions in this country—and its effect on my efforts to build a dependable community? Did I honestly think, dear father, that I had the energy or interest in overcoming all the barriers that I know I would have to negotiate in every relationship that I encountered in my new surroundings? In my state of low energy, lying on my bed at home during my convalescence, I could not honestly say that I was up for that kind of challenge in my later life.

I had used up a lot of enthusiasm getting established in my present academic position. That level of commitment could not be summoned once the motivation to do good in my career and be a success at my job was removed. I had to face the stark reality that I was on the other side of the steep career mountain. It was clear to me that my life had to have a different goal from here on into the future.

The other experience that set me thinking about my next chapter outside of teaching involved a friend who had survived several strokes. One day, he was painting his house, the next day, he was taken to the hospital and he did not wake up from a coma for six weeks. When K.W. did come back to consciousness, he was paralyzed down the left side of his body. That was the end of his career as a dancer, dance instructor, owner of his own dance school, performer who traveled around the world, costume designer, and tailor. I

met K.W. after his stay in the hospital and was moved to a senior living facility. We met when a friend escorted me to the residence hall to meet him. She was kind enough to arrange this introduction because I asked her to find out about the previous owner of two pieces of art that she gave to me as a gift. My friend told me that the pictures were sold at an estate sale that was staged at the home where K.W. once lived. His assets had to be liquidated so that all his money could be used to support him living in the community where he was established after coming out of the hospital. From our first meeting, I decided that I wanted to become part of K.W.'s support network and began to visit him every week. I committed to taking him a home-cooked meal regularly and spent time with him so I could learn about his career as a dancer and teacher.

Early in my journey with K.W., One of my colleagues told me that her daughters were once his students. This was long before he had the strokes that ended his teaching career. After seeing a DVD with a group of dances that he had choreographed for his students, I decided to ask him to choreograph a dance for me. It did not matter that I had not danced for decades. He took pity on me and he was kind enough to teach me once a week for at least two months. K.W. was a demanding teacher, and he quickly learned how to communicate his vision in dance movements as the weeks went by.

He was also coaching a young girl who wanted to enter a dance competition, so I got to see him interact with another student with a different dance style during my visits. I was amazed at what he got me to perform under his watchful eye. I was even more stunned at the patience that he exhibited as I learned to interpret his directions with more accuracy in every rehearsal.

At the end of these sessions, when we both felt that I had a piece that I could share with others, I decided to make a gift for K.W. This impulse was inspired by the kindness that this dance teacher showed me. As he faced the challenges of a lack of independence and reliance on medication to help him deal with the pain that his body was experiencing, K.W. never let the light of his love for dance ever dim in my presence.

One morning, I was in the shower, and I began humming the tune to "You've Got a Friend" by Carole King. This was a favorite song of my sister Debbie, and I kept hearing the melody in my head all day. I started to imagine a dance to this tune as I went about my chores. Since I have a lot of space in my living room, I cleared a section so I could do my choreography in the area.

I found a recording of the song that I liked—there was one by Carole King and her friend James Taylor. The live recording of them doing a duet suited the emotional intensity that I was feeling. Little by little, I created a piece that I felt K.W. could do in his wheelchair. Yes, Dad, he was going to dance in his wheelchair. The chair was going to do choreography. My imagination was on speed drive that day! I did not know if he would be willing to try to do the piece, or if he would even like what I created, I just knew that I wanted to give the dance to him. The point was that K.W. had inspired me to say something about our relationship after working together under very trying circumstances. He helped me to return to using the language of dance, which I had put aside for decades. Most of all, Dad, I wanted him to

feel appreciated and that would best be accomplished, I felt, by using the dance language that he knew well.

On the day of my final rehearsal with K.W., I told him that I had something to show him. I wanted his honest feedback, I said, while I set up my tape recorder to play the music of "You've Got a Friend." K.W. sat very still while I performed the piece. At the end of my presentation, he told me that it was "very good" and said that he would use it in a concert with his own dancers once he got a company together. I was deeply moved by his response. The dance was now his own, I explained, and he could do anything that he wanted to do with it. I also explained to him that he had to learn it. From now on, dear K.W. would be the student in our relationship.

This news did not faze him, or at least he did not let me know that it made him uneasy. From that day, in that rehearsal, we started collaborating on the piece. The dance changed in many ways, since K.W. was not able to get up from his chair without a lot of difficulty. He also did not have as much flexibility in the leg that he could move away from the chair. That did not stop him from creating the same feeling through his upper body movements as I had intended when I choreographed the dance. Our dance journey brought us together, gave us a sense of fulfillment, and created joy that we were both glad to share.

The result of this collaboration with K.W. and myself was a presentation in Trinidad for the prestigious Trinidad Theater Workshop. Tony Hall—you remember him? He was the first television director that I had when I was sixteen years old. He was the organizer of the series of shows that I was invited to appear in that season. The theater company

was featuring theater professionals with very long careers. I had the honor to do my dance for an audience that mostly knew me over forty years from the time that I was a dancer and actor in Trinidad. There were friends from high school, performers who I knew from my childhood, and many actors from productions that I had been involved with when I lived in Trinidad as a teen.

That evening I was able to do the dance, tell the story

of K.W.'s journey with me, and share my hopes for others to find a way to communicate in movement regardless of their physical capabilities. A few brave members from the audience joined me on the stage to learn the dance and perform it with me at my invitation. This interaction with the audience was lively and made me feel like I was being embraced by my own family. The end of the show was used for volunteers sharing feedback about their appreciation of my work with K.W. People were very positive about the dance and talked about the hope that it gave them for continuing to think about dance from a broader perspective.

We ended the evening with people talking to each other about the ways in which they now envisaged working with students, adults in the community, and those struggling with mental and physical challenges.

When I reported on the experience in Trinidad to K.W., there was only one regret on my part: I did not bring him a recording of the presentation. Even though I had asked for a copy of any film that was made on the evening of the show before I arrived in Trinidad, the producer did not want me to have a copy of the recording. There were plans to make a television series based on all the performances that the theater had featured over several months. I did not know

this was the plan when I accepted the invitation to perform at the theater. The result of this misunderstanding was that K.W. would not have the benefit of seeing the impact of his dance on the audience. I wanted my teacher and collaborator to hear the comments that people shared after listening to the story of our months together. It was important to me that he felt like he was there in the theater with us that evening. K.W. was understanding about the situation that I faced when I tried to get a copy of the film from the videographer.

It seemed a silly conflict to him. He knew that there were more important things to be upset about since his life was a challenge every day.

It turned out that the producer of that show died three years after I visited Trinidad. His sudden passing worked as another wake-up call to me and nudged me in the direction of understanding clearly how our final moments with friends and family are not easy to recognize. I questioned myself about the best possible way to use all the gifts that I had. The effort to get the producer of that show in Trinidad to let me see the recording of my performance and share it with K.W. prompted me to find a better way to spend my time on earth. What was the answer that my conscience was insisting that I seek out? Where would I find the means to make good use of the lessons that my time with K.W. taught me? The questions did not let up for months.

I keep looking for these answers, Dad. Your life reminds me that I can make good use of my time on earth. Even though you have been gone seventeen years, your voice still echoes in my heart. Your no-nonsense approach to your challenges shaped my attitude to the mountains that I had to climb to be successful. I still hear your laugh sometimes.

When I look at your picture that sits on the counter in my kitchen, I remember you calling me Joey. You were the only person who ever called me that name. It was decades before I heard someone else use that name, and it made me feel uncomfortable. That was your special name and no one else had permission to use it, right? Your fierce stance in the face of dealing with difficult relatives came back to me when I had to confront Mr. Kay. I was moved to channel your personality when I had to take care of business. Your lessons never went unheeded, Dad. When I was growing up, I never thought I would ever want to behave like you. But there I was —in a face-off with the landlord demanding that I get the service I was paying for. Yes, Lennox, you would have been proud of me. In fact, I know you are proud of me.

Please let me know that you are praying for me.

Yours,

Joey.

P.S. I forgot to tell you about the raccoons that were living in the attic of my new apartment. When I got out of the hospital with my pancreas still upset, I had to spend many nights listening to the family of nightcrawlers walking around in the space over my bedroom. Every night, I waited for the animals to fall into my bedroom and land on my bed on top of me. It felt like Mr. Kay had followed me to my new home so he could make me suffer for having the nerve to move out of his rental after standing up to him. Or, maybe it was a spirit reminding me that I had to make some serious changes in my life so my health would improve. It could be, Dad, that it was you up there, trying to tell me some important news from the other side. Smile.

A New Baby Well, Come

by Lin Bincle

Thank you for sharing in the wonder of this birth.

For expressing your care, concern,

love, happiness, and mirth.

We've all waited months to meet her,

and are anxious to see her smile,

but we know you won't mind us asking,

take precautions or wait a little while.

We know the intentions of your visit

really are the best,

but please remember both mother

and baby really need their rest.

And dad too, although very happy,

is also very tired.

Perhaps he'll seem a little gruff

or may easily be riled.

The baby—she is lovely,

and the mother is doing fine.

What they need most now

is comfort and just a little time.

The baby—you want to hold her,

but that's not always wise.

We all carry microbes

and then there is her size.

The baby—she is vulnerable.

Extra care really is a must.

And this brand new family

has much to readjust.

So when you finally visit,

be reasonable and brief.

Wash your hands. Don't cough.

Give the parents some relief.

We'll have a lifetime (God-willing)

to see this child grow.

So wait, watch, be patient.

Take things a little slow.

{ Lin Bincle, December 10, 1989, from the Chapel of St. John Hospital }

The Blue Tulip

by Don Truex

They say the Tulip never blooms blue,

As such is my love for you.

Though some might see me as a boarded up old house,

Deep inside burns with love so true there is no blue.

Only like the fireplace with embers that will not die,

fresh wood like thoughts of you

warm the scented room and sky.

Light glows softly across the dreams...,

I have a view,

The embers share a rainbow

like the thoughts I have of you.

The amber fireplace hues caressed by moonlight

streaming through the windows,

Stroke and warm our forms entwined

together in the trueness of love.

The uncommonness found only in true love

I share with you.

Fortunate are the few who seek no beyond.

Though raised by some, nourished, tended to by others,

Still untamed wild on shorelines and fields

In uncontrolled color,

It surrenders not its love and beauty for you

but to praise God.

They say the Tulip never blooms blue

Yet like my love for you,

Wild it grows, uncontrolled,

nourishing itself with thoughts of you.

Wild beauties yes...my love shares with you.

The Brotherhood Of Baseball

by Ben DiCola

Trust is the most elusive virtue of all. We trust the life partners we choose at the altar of matrimony. Yet, the divorce rate in America is well over 50 percent. We trust our siblings, our priests and ministers and even Uber drivers and pizza delivery boys. But all too often, they also have betrayed our trust. So, who can we place our trust in? Would you believe a baseball fan? While you chuckle and scoff at the notion of this, allow me to provide you with real life, first-hand examples.

On my most recent trip to Florida, I was dining at The Beach House on Bradenton Beach, when two Pittsburgh Pirates fans walked in. This was immediately recognizable by the Pirates' caps and shirts each man was wearing. The Pirates had played the Twins that day at LECOM Park. The team has called Bradenton their spring training home since 1969. I knew the game had been played, but I didn't know the outcome as my phone expired—having run out of minutes. So, I approached their table to find out the final score, assuming they had attended the game. They did. "The Pirates won, 1-0," one of them said. I immediately asked them, "Who pitched?" You need to realize if you are not a baseball fan, yet you are reading this book intently, that this is a most important question. If the final had been 6-2 or 8-3, then there would be no need to ask who pitched. But if the final tally is 1-0, that margin is paper thin, and the man who pitched takes center stage in terms of the game's importance. He held the opponent after all, scoreless.

"Chase De Jong," the other man noted. That's who pitched the 1-0 gem for the Pirates that day. De Jong didn't make the club coming out of spring training (considering the fate of the team's pitching staff, perhaps he should have!). A five-minute conversation between myself and the two men ensued, even though I had never seen these two men before, and they certainly did not know me. It's quite possible that I would have nothing in common at all with either man, other than the fact that we root for the same baseball team. That's it! Let's dissect this further, shall we?

Would you strike up a conversation with a total stranger because you both drive a pickup? Or an Equinox? Well, yes, you could. But it's far less likely, especially if you don't know the person at all. Would you go out of your way to talk to the person ahead of you in the grocery store checkout line, simply because he or she bought the same brand of orange juice or coffee that you purchased? Again, yes, you could. But, the other person would likely wonder why you are even asking. So, what? Where does the conversation go after you've established that each of you prefers Maxwell House coffee in cans?

But this exchange on Bradenton Beach with the Gulf of Mexico serving as a heavenly visual backdrop continued. Not only did we discuss De Jong's performance that day, we

also evaluated the Pirates' starting rotation overall, pitchers the team used to have that are now pitching elsewhere, the team's record in spring training, who is currently injured and cannot play, and when the first game of the season is scheduled. These questions and subsequent answers are expected. Nobody is taken aback by it. It is as though the three of us were all in the same high school graduating class.

We were not, of course, as I can readily surmise by looking at the two men that each is at least 20 years younger than I am. Maybe this is the "male bonding" concept we often hear about in reference to men. But, it's clear that because of baseball—and only because of it—that the three of us can engage in this non-planned, unrehearsed discourse.

To further illustrate the bond of baseball brotherhood, consider this transaction between myself and Shane Vecchio, a fellow Pirates' fan and a Pittsburgh resident. The power of social media has allowed the doors of friendship to swing wide open between us. I didn't know Shane from Moses or Joshua, but because of social media and the commonality of being Pirates' fans on a team page, we became friends.

It was my good fortune that Shane happened to have a rare 1960 Pirates' World Series program when Pittsburgh upset the heavily favored New York Yankees that fall. He posted it online and was willing to accept a sale to the first responder. Turned out to be me! I asked Shane how much he wanted for the storied program that went for .50 cents over six decades ago. His asking price was $125. He told me it remained in good condition.

Now, here is where the formidable bond of trust comes in. If you haven't already figured this out, it became clear that Shane had to trust a person like me, a person he has never seen or met, to mail him a check for $125. I, on the other hand, also had to trust someone I had never met—a person I only knew through a computer screen—to send me what he claimed was a 1960 Pirates' World Series program that he further confirmed was in 'good condition.' We exchanged a few messages centered on this point, but we both knew the other was going to come through with his end of the bargain. How did we know that?

We knew because baseball fans have an unshakable foundation, a firm resolve that comes from a lifelong loyalty of following a sports team, good or bad, successful or not. Would I trust anyone else with a transaction online? No, I would not. Why not? Because the brotherhood of man isn't attached to it. The bond of trust doesn't exist.

The 1960 World Series program was indeed in very good condition. Shane Vecchio did indeed receive his $125 from me. What he did with it is his business. I know what I did with the program (no, it is not in the bathroom!).

It rests comfortably on the first shelf of my Pirates' baseball shrine in my sports den. The ads in the program are as startling as the content. One message advertises Schick razor blades. Another promotes Philco radios, now available in stereo!

There are highlights of the Pirates' 1960 season, a picture of Dodgers' pitcher Don Drysdale lunging to tag Pirates' shortstop Dick Groat, and a full history of the World Series players' shares in previous years. I didn't know which was more shocking to the eye; the fact that the year before in 1959, that the individual players' winning share on the Los

Angeles Dodgers was $11,231.18, or that there was a full page congratulatory ad honoring the 1960 Pirates from the Republican presidential ticket that year—Richard Nixon and Henry Cabot Lodge!

All I know for sure is that trust can still thrive between people. Being a baseball fan may not be the only way to achieve it, but without question, it's an excellent start!

The Caribbean and COVID-19

by Joanne Kilgour Dowdy

I found this prompt for a journal article in a professional site and decided that I would write a personal response rather than a research report as the editors requested:

How has the Caribbean been coping? What has been the impact on the people, including the children? What are some of the successful strategies employed by the various governments? What are the implications for tourism, the economy, education, online learning? How has it affected gender-based violence? How has it influenced our interaction and engagement, now and going forward? What are the lessons to be learned?

A formal article would not do, I told myself. I would prefer to describe the experiences that I have endured since March 2020. How else to communicate the heartache that this year created? I was trained to believe that the personal is political. This has led to me thinking that if something is happening to me, to my loved ones, it must be result of decisions made at another level in my existence. If a government makes a decision that leads to people taking certain measures to protect themselves, then it follows that I will see those effects in different places that I carry on my daily activities. How the COVID-19 pandemic has affected me and my extended family over the last year is a good measure of the political realities that impact our lives. Some examples of interactions with Caribbean people in the USA and overseas, in Trinidad, Jamaica, and Barbados, help me to illustrate my lived experience since March 2020.

When I was sent home to "shelter in place" last year, I was anticipating the arrival of my retirement from teaching at Kent State University. The fact that I would be teaching from home, online, only meant that I would not have to face the hassle of getting dressed every morning and facing the horrible winter weather that we are blessed to endure every March. Preparing lessons for my students and interacting with them every day seemed to be a "reward" for the long years that I had labored in a classroom. Up close and personal now had a new meaning for me.

Not a fan of online teaching, reluctant to embrace the technology, but still curious enough to offer a hybrid course the previous two years, I was up for the challenge when the pandemic sent us all scurrying for safety. I had no idea, and no one else did at the time, that this would be the new normal for teaching college students. I reveled in the fact that I finished my time on campus two months early and would also have my retirement "celebration" online. The campus was now history to me. I was starting my new life with bells and whistles in my ears.

My Aunt G. has a gardener who has worked for her over the last twenty years. He calls her every night to make sure that she is safe. If she tells him of anything that causes him to be concerned for her safety, he takes a bus to her house and checks that everything is secure before he leaves for home. This dear man, a life saver if there ever was one, has no regular income. As a result of the COVID-19 protocol, people are not working, and they are not hiring workers. Unfortunately, the families who once paid this gardener to take care of their lawns and flower beds cannot afford to pay him for his services. It seems that several people are waiting until he arrives at their home to tell him that his services are not wanted. This means that he has paid $400, in his currency, to take a bus to the address and then return home. His daily wage does not cover the expense of transportation. What is this devoted worker to do in this time of the pandemic chaos? If it is happening to him, it is happening to thousands of daily wage earners. The personal is a result of the decisions made by people who govern their country so that every citizen feels safe and can prosper.

A group of my high school friends started meeting on Zoom and enjoyed the exchanges so much that they made a commitment to visit with each other once a month. These friends lived in Trinidad, Barbados, Jamaica, Washington, D.C., and Texas. They were not interested in sending out lots of invitations, even though they enjoyed being on a chat with graduates of the same high school in Trinidad. This group kept up with each other, celebrated birthdays online, and made sure that they passed on news of deaths that might be of interest to anyone who had been in high school with us over forty years ago. There was a lot of catching up on each person's lives in the meetings that I attended. Certainly, I was happy to see people I had not set eyes on for more than forty years since I first left Trinidad to study in the U.S.A.

I understood how far each of us had traveled as I listened to the hurdles that people had jumped in their quest to be successful in the discipline that they followed as a career. We had a scientist with a doctorate in Jamaica, a psychologist who taught on campus in Barbados, two retirees in Texas and Ohio in the USA, a business owner in Maryland, and a retired public school teacher in Trinidad. This was the result of the pandemic in the Caribbean: very old friends had time to visit and to hear about other people's lives. It took a global plague to allow people the space to visit with each other using technology. Without this health challenge that affected every country in the world, the gathering of friends from high school would be possible. We would not otherwise have had a chance to check in with each other after many decades.

The downside of this monthly meeting of friends on Zoom is that they have to end the meeting and go back to the reality of sheltering in place or being in a lockdown mandated by their local government. The isolation is hard to cope with after being in a mostly enjoyable meeting with people you have known for over forty years of your life. I find that the silence around me is harder to cope with after the Zoom meeting than when I was moving around the house, feeling like I am in a bubble, making myself busy with tasks that take up lots of time before I get back into bed at night.

I haven't talked to other people on the Zoom meeting about this fact, but I am reflecting on the kind of comments that I share with my aunt when I call her in Jamaica. She cannot go outside to visit her neighbor, is not allowed to go to the bank and do her important monthly transactions, is not allowed to have guests come into her home, and on and on and on. She is bored and she doesn't know how much more of this kind of isolation is possible for her to tolerate. It does not help that I tell her I am under the same kind of restrictions and that I am worse off since I have no one living with me. Her phone is her saving grace because she can talk to relatives in Trinidad, Canada, and the U.S.A.

Aunt Bea is a gregarious person and feels that it's cruel and unusual punishment to make an old woman sit still all day long with no visitors coming to keep her company. People must stand at the end of the driveway and call out to her when they come to visit. She stays on the front porch and shouts out to them for the duration of the visit. Packages are left on the end of the porch for her to pick up after the guest has departed. Her young friends take every precaution to let her see that they are being mindful of the protocol in place to keep her safe from catching the virus. This is just painful for my aunty—now ninety-five years old—and she can't imagine how much longer she will be able to put up with the whole dance of the virus protocol.

Sheltering in place means that my friend Salle has lots of time to paint and clean the weeds in her garden. She sends photos from her computer when she gets images of the poui trees blossoming on the hills in Trinidad. Salle also sent me a painting of a church in Macqueripe that she "imagined" based on the history that she was able to gather about the venue that free slaves built. I learned from this artist, a retiree from the banking industry in Trinidad, that the Americans once occupied this part of Trinidad during World War II. I ask myself if Salle had taken the time to do this painting before the pandemic. It is possible that she would have spent time painting, but maybe not with such a concentrated effort as she has been reporting over the years. I know that my friends always approached her painting as a hobby until now. Salle paints in spurts of effort, as the mood takes her, and this enforced time of quiet has given her the mental space to focus on the images that fascinate her. The painting habit is now therapy that has saved her from feeling abandoned by family and friends who cannot visit her in her home.

A friend of mine left Trinidad in October, 2020, to visit and help her daughter with a newborn baby in Canada. Nagee gave notice to her employers that she did not know when Trinidad would let her reenter the country. It was understood that she could work remotely, and therefore, she was busy teaching online the whole time that she was overseas. She had to stay in Barbados on her return trip to Trinidad since the borders were closed at home. When she was finally allowed to return to Trinidad, she had to stay in a hotel for two weeks.

Then, she was told to stay home and keep to herself for a week after her release from the hotel. In all, she was gone from her job and teaching online from October 2020 to March 2021. It was her great fortune that her grandchild arrived safely in Canada, and Nagee was able to help her daughter for the first three months of the child's arrival during the winter.

When Nagee landed in Barbados, she was again fortunate to have another daughter put her up for the short visit that was forced on her due to Trinidad's stringent restrictions on arriving passengers. How many people can afford to stay away from their jobs that long? How many have the support system in place to allow them to "airport hop" from the Caribbean to Canada and back, while they wait for a government to let them enter their home country? Another case of the impact of the quarantine that countries are enforcing reminds me of my aunt's son and his visit to Jamaica last December. He had to take care of business that would affect his ability to keep my aunt in her home. Risking his life and knowing that his mother would be upset if she did not see him while he was on the island he went to Jamaica.

Deva stayed in quarantine at a hotel for two weeks while he took care of business with his lawyer. His whole vacation was spent sheltering in place, and the fun times that he always enjoyed in Jamaica were canceled from his annual vacation. When he finally went to see his mother, he had to stay six feet away from her and keep his mask in place. My aunt could not believe what she had to endure the day of his visit.

I had to hear about it several times and the fact that everyone is observing these protocols has not diminished her outrage about the situation. Every week, my aunt complains about being under "house arrest" and complains bitterly that she does not know when next she will see her son. He was supposed to retire this year, but under the pandemic circumstances, it doesn't look like he will be returning to Jamaica in the near future. What does the COVID- 19 pandemic mean for grieving the loss of loved ones? A cousin in Toronto lost his wife suddenly after she complained that she was not feeling well one night. In two weeks, she succumbed to the fourth stage cancer that had overtaken her abdomen. His family was mostly in Canada, but they could not attend the funeral.

This is the song that has continued to play throughout the year of the virus spreading all over the world. In Jamaica, another cousin arranged to have my elderly aunt visit his home where she could observe the funeral that was taking place in Canada. It was a "command performance" she told me, and she had to be a witness to that ceremony with or without the virus protocols in place. My rage at the fact that she left her home and risked being infected by visiting her nephew and his family did not make a dent in her self-righteous attitude. Family is more important than any government restrictions on the public, she had me understand. We have to do what we have to do.

She also sang the praises of the technology that would allow her to sit in a home in Jamaica and see a funeral in Canada. Well, the only problem for her was the fact that she could not speak at the funeral. She had to sit still; with her limited eyesight, it meant being right in front of the screen and listening to the comments that her nephew and great nieces made about their mother. What does shelter in place mean to me after these twelve months? It means a quiet time to write my memoir. It means reaching out to friends who I have not heard from or remembered for decades. Like the email that I got from a school teacher I met at the Holy Name Convent Secondary School. I could not believe I was seeing my music teacher's name on the list of email messages I pulled up on my screen. When I got in touch with her by phone, she was elated that I remembered her, and that I chose to reach out to her.

Mrs. Rose wanted me to give her directions about getting a book published. I had lots to say on that topic, and she was pleased that I was so willing to share my experiences with publishing books. It would take a lot of imagination from me to come up with an idea for a teacher who was in my life over forty years before, would contact me to get advice about her writing career. This pandemic has become a mystery and a puzzle wrapped up in an enigma.

Another aunt fell and hit her head out in the backyard at her house. She was alone and had to go to the public hospital to find out if she had damage inside her skull. When the doctor saw the images from the x-rays, she found out that she had an infection in her head. She has no pension, and her former husband died a year before this accident. There was no alimony coming to her this year. I decided to find a way to get money to her so she could pay for the hospital bill and buy medication. This set the Caribbean informal banking system in motion. I called a friend in Canada to ask if she could deliver cash to my aunt in exchange for a check, which I would put in the mail that week. She thought that we could find someone closer to my aunt so the money would be in her hands sooner and the medication could start immediately. I called another friend in Trinidad who owns a pharmacy and arranged with him to deliver cash to my aunt immediately. Yes, the money was there that week and my aunt got someone to pick up the payment at the pharmacy. We solved the problem through collective action. The social network is in place and it works when all members of the group are willing to do their part.

Our ancestors, I am happy to realize, gave us a system that we could use in all ages and under all circumstances. The community all across the globe is always a phone call away in times of need. The deaths of family and friends have been piling up. The first notice of a loved one succumbing to heart disease came in April. It took a year before I could summon the courage to look at the memorial that was posted online a week after his death in Trinidad. I have been waking up with images of this friend and mentor in my mind for the last week. Another death notice came in when a friend from high school died after receiving surgery and then getting the virus before he left the hospital. It was November, 2019—the day of my birthday—that we last saw each other at a ceremony in Washington, D.C. I could not join his wife and family for a funeral ceremony because flights were not a good idea before we got vaccinations.

Then, there was the sudden death of my aunt's dear friend of sixty years one Sunday morning in Jamaica. She was driving herself to the hospital when she had a heart attack. This woman was famous for her work with the national floral society in Jamaica. Only five people could attend the ceremony that her niece and nephew organized. I have learned over the last year that calling and talking to people who are in grief just does not seem to hit the right note for helping them deal with their loss. My aunt tells me that she breaks down and cries every time that she remembers her friend.

Joining online writing groups has opened up my world to writers from Canada and other parts of the United States. I have a meeting every two weeks with one group and another meeting with the group founded in Ohio. In both groups, I am the only person from the Caribbean. In the group from Ontario, I am the only black person who meets every session.

My responses to the writing prompts are unique to my experience of growing up in Trinidad. The prompts for writing lead me to describe tropical scenes while the other writers recall snowy days and French lessons at their public school. My childhood friends are from African, Indian, and Chinese ancestors. Some of them, like me, have elders who come from all three backgrounds. I also bring a black female voice to addressing the issues of integration and immigration.

The pandemic has delivered this blessing of finding out how many ways that human beings are similar. Yet, I am so happy that a writer who is originally from a part of India has joined the Ontario meeting. I prefer not to be the "one" who is non-white in the group. My feelings about being the raisin in the cream are always on the surface of my perspective. It may also be, as my friend in Trinidad has told me, that this long year of isolation has made me more extreme in my reactions of happiness and sadness.

For the last ten years, I have celebrated the winner of the Kathleen Armstrong Kilgour Dance Scholarship Award with the teachers and faculty at the Caribbean School of Dancing in Trinidad. In 2020, we had to do the ceremony online, since the winner of the award was in quarantine in Trinidad, and the director of the dance company that chose the award winner was in Canada. I, one of the donors of the scholarship, was in Ohio. Jaye was already on scholarship studying musical theater at a school in New York when she got the news that we would do the presentation on Zoom.

Jaye was in Trinidad on the day of the presentation, while the director of the Metamorphosis Dance Company was in Canada with her daughter and I was in Ohio, waiting to do the formal speech after the award was announced.

Dancers from the company and teachers from the dance school in Trinidad were online for the Zoom meeting, and everyone who could find a computer to join our celebration offered their congratulations to the winner after the announcement. This was a strange event, since we did not get to hand over the bouquet of flowers that each winner of the scholarship award was given at the event.

The announcement usually takes place during a rehearsal at the dance school with the dance company members, and the presenter of the award is someone from the dance community or one of the donors of the scholarship. I was happy to meet Jaye online, but it felt very uncomfortable to see her come to tears alone in a room where she could not turn to her fellow dancers and hug them as they cheered and enthusiastically applauded her. I was reminded by the small number of participants in that ceremony that not everyone in the dance company could afford a computer or get to a computer so that they could be part of the event.

I have had the gift of time to write during these thirteen months of sheltering in my home. The memoir that I longed to begin when I was still teaching on campus is now in its third draft. I have plans to finish this book in June this year. Then, I will share it with a friend who once taught me in a college course on literature from African women. Looking back over the year will feel like a good, long drink after a walk in the desert. My soul is being fed by these quiet days of reflection on the journey from 1995 to 2020. I don't know of any other author with my background in theater and television who has penned such a book.

Nobody could have guessed that I would be forced to stay in my house and find constructive ways to use my time. No one could have made me sit still almost every day for those months and write over 200 pages for my new book. The pandemic drama is unfolding before my eyes as I type these words and realize that I am safe—I have food, friends, and a future in publication. So many thousands have no positive outcome for the trouble that they have endured in 2020 and may continue to face in 2021 and beyond. Am I happy to have my book in draft form? Some days, it sustains me to keep writing. Other days, I caution myself not to go around boasting about my accomplishments since retirement. Everyone isn't doing well under these dire constraints that the virus threat has dictated.

In the newspaper article that I got published in the Trinidad Express last year, I talked about my commitment to deepening my spiritual practice in meditation and study. This effort did not come easily in the early months of the lock down. The idea had to come to me as I realized that there was going to be a lot of hours spent in seclusion and I had better make good use of the quiet. I am not a person who watches television regularly. Nor am I interested in spending lots of time on the phone. A friend of mine in Dakar, Senegal, told me that she wondered how I was making out with this long journey under virtual house arrest since I was not a phone person. Well, I have taken the opportunity to be more disciplined about my time in the meditation room. I read a lot more literature from my faith community. The radio provides me with programs from pastors who teach methods for studying the Bible, and these lessons are eye-openers since I did not spend time listening to Christian sermons after I left high school.

I am in school while I am sheltering from the virus and its deadly effects. When I open my eyes in the morning, I start by saying thanks to my Maker for keeping me alive.

I am even more grateful that my friends and family are still living. I now appreciate my grandmother for making sure that her children and grandchildren remembered to give thanks for life every day. When my feet touch the ground and my eyes open, I say a thankful prayer to my Maker for getting me to another day safely.

My friend Carol, from Jamaica, contacted me through email and then arranged a visit on Zoom. It was nineteen years since we had seen each other. We talked like we had never lost touch with each other and had to laugh at the fact that we were still troubling the political questions that helped us bond when we first met in Atlanta. After several weeks of corresponding, I asked Carol to help me find a program that taught choreography. She graciously decided to teach me online for six weeks. This experience has been life-changing, since I have not danced in a class for almost 20 years. We created a short piece based on a chapter from the memoir that I am writing. By the end of the six weeks, we were both wondering about continuing our collaboration. It did not matter to us that she was in Boston and I was in Ohio. Our Caribbean backgrounds made it easy for us to communicate about our artistic visions and the way we wanted to proceed with the dance piece.

Almost simultaneously, we both decided that we wanted to invite a mutual friend who was teaching at the Berklee school of music in Boston. I suggested that Carol get in touch with this musician from Trinidad and tell him about our work over six weeks and our ambitions for the future of our project.

It turns out that this Caribbean musician from Trinidad was ready to join in our Zoom journey to create an original piece that represented the chapter from my memoir. I could not have wished for a more perfect union of minds and hearts to work on my dance and help me speak to the heart of it. Jamaica and Trinidad are represented in this collaboration that will be shared with the world later in the year. It is another gift of the global pandemic that no one could have imagined happening.

I have been attending classes on Hindu scripture conducted by the Vedanta Center of St. Petersburg in Florida twice a week. This is a site that I visited in 2019 and made up my mind to spend summers nearby so that I could enjoy the members and the leader of the center in person. Since we are now doing online classes, I have the pleasure of listening to the lectures every week without going to Florida and finding a place to stay for an extended visit. This temporary arrangement hasn't deterred me from dreaming of the day when I can find a summer rental and have the luxury of going to the center to enjoy these lectures and the company of the members at that site.

What is obvious to me when I look at the pictures of people who sign on for classes every week is that I am bringing a Caribbean voice to the assembly. I may be wrong, but I don't see any faces on the screen that make me think that I may be among a group of people who include someone from my background. Trinidad, where I grew up, has a population that is almost fifty percent Indian descendants.

Many of my friends in primary and secondary school claimed Indian ancestors. My best friend in elementary school had a Chinese father and Indian mother. Roxanne looked Chinese, but she never claimed that she was Chinese to anyone who asked about her parents and heritage. The classes at the center are another place that the global pandemic has led me to expand my social circle. My presence at that site provides a window on the world that I would not have otherwise. Going to class lets me see different people from my usual social network and allows them to see me as part of a larger interest group than would otherwise be in their wheelhouse.

If my plans for retirement had worked out as I imagined, then I would not have been in one place for many weeks at a time. Travel out of state and overseas was supposed to dominate my itinerary for the first months free of teaching every week. Since I was grounded like the rest of the world, I decided to join the League of Women Voters and keep up with their meetings all through the year that COVID-19 protocols had us sheltering in place. The virtual meetings were organized for committees to do work that encouraged people to get out and vote for the 2020 elections. I met people who would otherwise not have been in my social circle and, therefore, not part of the important experience of sharing mutual interests about voters' rights.

Again, I am in the minority on these dates when I meet with members of the organization. I have only seen one non-white person at any of the sessions that I have attended. It amazes me that we are in the twenty-first century and it is still possible to enter spaces where the majority white population is so well represented. Is it that non-white people still will not trust predominantly white organizations and so they don't get involved with the work?

Or maybe the organizations don't do enough outreach activities to encourage the folks who are marginalized to get involved if they share mutual interests. I told a friend who encouraged me to join the LWV that I turn up to meetings to find out what is going on in the county. It's my fault if I don't make the effort to be a part of the push to improve our voter turnout and stop the extreme level of gerrymandering that has affected our state.

The pandemic has delivered many gifts in the last year. I must admit, this visit with my aunt on the phone is the most precious of all the memories that will remain with me. When I finally outlive the sheltering in place, and can look back at the year that we all hid in our homes to be protected from the deadly virus, I will remember how the government decided to protect all of us. It will also be clear to me that my aunt was spared a lot of suffering since she had to stay inside and let people come to the house to help her. Her family came together to make her life safe and happy. I must tip my hat to the government that made a decision to keep the whole county safe. We all had to accept what we could not change. No one that I know can stay upset about the inconvenience that we had to endure for the greater good.

When I want to complain about the way in which my plans for retirement were changed—and not in a happy way —I will be forced to remember that I got a lot out of being confined in my home. As my grandma always told us, "It's better to be safe than sorry." Better words could not be said about the journey during the year of the global pandemic.

My aunt in Jamaica has quit asking me when I am going to come see her. This week, she asked me to write a letter on her behalf and send it out to the family. I have asked her to let me publish this letter as part of my chapter. You can see what changes have taken place in her life since COVID-19 forced her to stay inside, stop visiting her friends, and make peace with the fact that she had to rely on the phone more than she already was doing before the pandemic changed all of our lives.

April 22, 2021.

Dear Family and Friends:

I pray that you and your family are happy, healthy, and safe. I wanted to reach out and let you know how I have been doing over the last year.

First, I want to thank you for your loving support of my recovery since my bout with pneumonia in 2019. Many of you called and sent messages to me so that I would be encouraged on the long journey to good health. Some of my friends came by and spent time with me and I deeply appreciate their loving concern.

My doctor has insisted that I have caretakers staying with me all day. They insist that if I get sick or have some emergency that I cannot handle, someone should be here to help me.

Right now, I have been blessed with two caring and professional ladies who look after me. It so happened that an old friend from Nestle got in touch with me and recommended these two helpers. One of them, Ann, comes in during the day and she makes sure that I have breakfast and lunch. Ann Marie, who some of you know, still comes in on two days. She takes care of many personal businesses and makes sure that I have food and medicine in the house. My second caretaker, Lorna, has many credentials to her name and is a very loving person. Both the ladies who have been coming in the last month are a blessing to my life. I feel that "the man upstairs" is looking out for me just as my son, Roger, always promised me.

Since the COVID-19 pandemic began last year, I have had to remain in the house and protect myself from catching the virus. I thank my Maker that my doctor got me signed up for a vaccination and I have already got the first dose. I have not been allowed to walk down the street and visit with my neighbors. I have not been able to take a taxi and go visit my close friend every week. We used to enjoy the time together while we talked about life and our old friends. That change in my schedule has been very hard for me since I am alone so much of the day. My friend Yvonne calls every morning and reads a prayer to me. I enjoy listening to music on the radio since it is quite soothing. It is wonderful that I can call family and friends and spend lots of time on the phone talking about the changes that this pandemic is causing.

Once again, thank you very much for your support of my journey over the last two years. My health has improved significantly, and I continue to make progress every day. I am convinced that your loving concern has made the difference in my overall well-being. Please feel free to call and chat with me. Your calls mean the world to me during these long days when I am not allowed to visit friends in person. I look forward to seeing some of you in person when this virus is under control.

Yours sincerely,

Aunty

I wrote this letter, after recording two conversations with my Aunty, and sent it out to family under the strong impression that my aunt was saying farewell to all of us. It may be the last time that we have such an intimate conversation about her experiences. She is on tape since I wanted to record her voice as she told me about the good luck that she is experiencing with the two women who take care of her every day. I have a record of her voice cracking as she tells me of the old friend from her last job who came to visit her, and promised that she would find people to take care of her, and she should not worry anymore. She can't believe that this woman remembered her after so many years since she retired from her job of almost 40 years. It's clear to me that I will be replaying this recording for many years after my aunt passes on.

Caught Between Trains

by James Valentino

There they were, the two of them, sitting on a bench at the old Cleveland Union Depot while their train whistled in the distance as it sped on westbound without them. Rob offered Leslie a cigarette, which she shook her head no to as she looked up at the clock on the wall. It was seven-thirty in the evening in Cleveland, Ohio. They would have gone on to Chicago but if they did, there wouldn't have been a nickel left between them. So, here they were—in Rob's hometown, wondering what they had to do next.

She finally spoke. "The sun is setting."

He looked at her. "I told you not to come."

"We're in this together, remember?"

"Well, we are now." He stood up and yawned. "We got to get out of here."

They only had four bucks left between them, so, instead of taking a cab, they walked up East Ninth Street to the heart of downtown. They spot a diner across from Short Vincent, which was already hopping as the sun was setting. They walked up to the counter and the guy working there came over.

"What will it be?"

Rob glanced at the paper menu in front of him. "How about two coffees and maybe a roll?" The guy went and grabbed a roll in the back and poured them their coffees. "You take milk?" he asked Leslie.

"Yes, please."

"I'll go get some."

"By the way, do you have a paper?" Rob asked.

"There might be some in the newsstand out front." They walked right past it without noticing.

"I'll get one." Leslie went out to put some change in the thing and there was one left. The Cleveland Press, April 16, 1933 it said on the top. When she came back in, Rob already grabbed the table next to the window. He split the roll and gave her half while she handed him the paper except for the ads.

"Thanks." He glanced at the front page and saw nothing to worry about. Still, he'd feel safer once they hit Frisco.

"Do you think we can get a room for the night?" she asked as he looked at page two. Rob put down the paper and looked at her. "Perhaps we can get one. Won't be the Hollenden Hotel, but something." He smiled at her. "I think we'll be okay."

"Oh, I know we will, but I want to know what's going on Rob." He lit a cigarette and got up. "Can you hold on for an hour?"

"Why?"

"Just give me an hour." He turns to the guy at the counter. "Is Charley's still around?" That was a bar   turned speakeasy nearby.

"Yeah," the man said.

"Good." He leaned down and kissed Leslie's cheek. "Just give me one hour."

"Okay," was all she could say, and by the tone of her voice, it sounded like she didn't have much confidence in what he was up to.

As he left the diner and walked north on East Ninth, he started to whistle a tune. After all, he could hustle a few bucks in a pool game and that can help with getting a room. Besides, he had to get away from Leslie and think. It seemed so much longer than thirteen hours ago that he called her up at her place, frantic, at six-thirty in the morning. What could he tell her, that he had to get out of New York because he saw a guy get shot and recognized the one who killed him? He wasn't even supposed to be at that place where it happened, but he promised Carl he'd finish up; and so, at five in the morning, on the Lower East Side, this mess happened.

He was just telling her goodbye on that phone but by the time the call was over, Leslie told him she'd meet him at the station—which is exactly what she did, with a suitcase in hand. From what he saw in the paper, there was no news of it here, but the sooner they reached the West Coast, the safer he'd feel.

An hour later, as promised, Leslie saw Rob waving at

her from the other side of the window before he entered the

diner again. He took nine dollars out of his pocket and put it on the table. She quickly slipped the bills in her purse so no one saw them.

"What did you do?" Leslie asked.

"Got into a pool game and won twenty-five.

"That's wonderful," she smiled.

"Of course, I lost fifteen, so you just put away the difference." Still, it was nine more dollars to the good, and the two he realized he still had in his pocket. She showed him the newspaper with check marks next to the hotels and rooms she felt were in their budget, not many but good for a day or two.

"Why a room now that we can get two bus tickets to Chicago?" He asked her. "Do we have enough for both?" Rob let out a yawn. "I guess, but not much else. Besides, I still want to get out to Frisco."

"So we might as well spend a night here."

"Okay, then we might as well grab some supper." He whistled for a waitress to come over and ordered two meatloaf specials.

Based on the limited choices Leslie checked off in the newspaper, they got a room at a broken-down hotel for their nights for four bucks. It was a regular size room with an actual bathroom—if you can call it such— and windows overlooking the street. He sat on the side of the bed, then dropped backward, exhausted. She looked out the window at the busy street. "What am I doing here?" she asked herself, knowing full well what the answer was.

"Are you going to see your family?" she asked.

"No," he replied immediately and rolled on his side, his feet still touching the floor.

"Maybe you should."

"Why don't you call your old man, honey?" The old buzzard must still be on that ranch out in Wyoming.

"Never." Not after what he used to do to her.

"As long as they don't find us, we'll be fine."

She turned around and looked at him. "Rob, you never really told me what happened." He opened his blue-gray eyes and raised his head a bit. "And I ain't going to tell you." It was sunrise when he opened his eyes again to see his girlfriend sitting in the one chair across from him.

"Good Morning," she greeted him with a smile and a different dress on.

"What time is it?"

"Almost ten."

He rubbed his head. "I really must have needed the rest."

"Now you know why I didn't disturb you."

"What did you do?"

"Napped a little, too, and there's a Woolworth's down

the street, so I got a few things." She only spent around a dollar. After all, things like toothpaste and a brush didn't cost that much. Rob sat up on the bed and stretched.

"Breakfast?"

"If there's a thirty-cent special around, perhaps we can."

"Later on, I think I can come up with some more dough." He gets up and goes into the small bathroom. She heard the sound of water running.

"Hustling pool?"

"Yeah, by hustling pool—unless we plan to stay here, which I don't." He came back out wiping his face with a small towel.

As they went out, Rob wondered if Wally picked up on his scent. His big brother always seemed to show up wherever he was growing up, even when he wasn't wanted. Sure enough, when they walked out of the Colonial Arcade, a cop car pulled up next to him on the street with the window rolled down. It was him.

"What the hell are you doing here?" Officer Walter Kozak asked his kid brother.

"Good morning, nice to see you too."

"When did you come in?"

"Yesterday," if that was any of his business.

The officer finally glanced at his brother's girlfriend,

"Hi, I'm Rob's brother." She smiled at him, "Nice to finally meet you."

"Leslie Adams," Rob finally introduced her.

"Plan to call up pop?"

"You can tell him I'm here."

"We haven't heard from you in two months. Aunt Margo was getting worried."

"Well, Wally, now you can tell them you saw me." Rob started to walk but his brother just coasted the car in pace with him.

"Where are you staying?"

"I got a room."

Wally looked at Leslie. "I know that, but what's the address? Maybe I can stop by later?"

"How about I call you?" The last thing he wanted was Wally stopping over.

"Dolly and I got a new place out on Eddy Road." Dolly, or Dolores, was Wally's wife of three years. He took out his pad and wrote the phone number down. "Here," he ripped the page out and handed it to his brother. "Call me tonight."

"Sure", Rob looked at the paper until his girlfriend took it and put it in her purse.

"Nice meeting you," she told Wally.

He reached out and shook her hand. "Same here, Miss Adams."

"Bye Wally," Rob wanted to send him on his way. With that, Office Kozak drove off. As they walked down the street, she heard Rob mutter more to himself, "I knew we should have bought bus tickets to Toledo."

Later that night, he hustled another game at Charley's and won six more bucks, but that wasn't enough to live on, let alone get out of there. Yet, he had to think of making money from something else and at a different place so he didn't become a regular, and a nuisance. While doing a hole in one, Rob did notice that the piano was silent. The guy playing it yesterday was nowhere to be found. If Leslie wasn't expecting him, he would have asked the bartender if they needed a player for the night. Then again, Rob knew he could do a lot better than a pool hall—but places like the Hotel Cleveland didn't need musicians by the hour. As he headed back, his mind moved on to other things. Should he ask Wally to lend him money?

He looked for gigs in the paper, but Cleveland was just as bad off in the job market as the East Coast. All his skills tend to land him in jail, which was why for the past few years, he used them sparingly. He could tend bar at a speakeasy, but not here—not with his brother the cop around. Yet, even if he could get a full-time job, he sure didn't want one here.

To think that he first went to the Big Apple thinking he could apply at Julliard. That seemed like ages ago, though it was only 1928. He was working back then, playing the organ at the Keith 105th up at Doan's Corners for the movies until they went all Talkies and he was out of a job. Once again, not wanting to work at the mill with his pop, and with the whole world before him, or so it seemed, Rob hopped on a train for New York City and thought he wouldn't have to look back. Boy, a lot of things happened in the five years since then.

While waiting for him to come back, Leslie had time to finally think about everything, and what to do next. There were friends she could call—a lot of male friends wondering what happened to her—some girls from the shows she used to be in, or the department store, which she was at until two days ago. Rubie was the only one of the entire bunch she would even think of calling if the situation was as bad as she believed it was, but after that one call at the diner, Leslie left her alone. If she only stopped to think yesterday morning when he called. Right now, she could still be in her apartment on Riverside Drive.

Then again, she could be right now in some police station being interrogated for something she still didn't really know, and for weeks afterward, worrying about them following her every move. Whatever the case, Leslie knew that if she stayed back there, she would never see him again, no matter how much he'd want to contact her.

It started to dawn on her that they would be there more than a few days. That revelation changed everything for her. They had to find better lodgings, ones she felt his brother would approve of. That would take some money, and there went the bus, let alone train tickets. Leslie realized she had to do something. She hated just being there, not helping out. Sometimes it was easier for a girl to get part-time jobs, so Leslie decided to look over the want ads in the paper. She knew how to type, and was a good one, too. And, sure enough, there were a couple of ads for a typist; not much, but enough for what they planned to do. Circling a few of them, she went downstairs to the phone and made some calls.

Rob got back to the hotel frustrated. Leslie was there to greet him. "Got some work."

"Huh?" She showed him the ad for a temporary typist.

"It's for a week, but that can get us to Frisco—probably."

"How much?"

"Fifteen dollars."

"Fifteen, yeah if we don't eat anything for a week we can get there, and sleep on a park bench."

"Well, it sure beats hustling pool." She was getting angry.

"Do you want to stay here?" he asked incredulously.

"I don't know, I only wish you'd tell me everything."

"So that's it," He smoothed his blond hair with his left hand. "The less you know, the better. Believe me."

"No Rob, it just makes me more worried." A minute later, he cleared his throat and came over to her. "I'm happy you snagged that job."

"Are you?"

"Sure," he put his arms around her waist, "Together, we'll manage somehow."

"You think you can win enough in a few days to buy two tickets?"

"Maybe." He sat with her on the edge of the bed. "At least enough to get a nicer room in the meantime." She looked into his eyes, "You're right, I don't think we will be leaving here anytime soon."

"I didn't say that."

"You don't have to." She picked up today's newspaper that way on the floor and pointed out all the circles he made earlier in the want ads.

"Well, you can only make dough from playing pool for so long."

She nodded her head, "We probably can get two bus tickets to Chicago with this."

"I was just thinking the same thing. Maybe even Denver."

"As long as we're together Robbie."

He drew her to him and kissed her. She kissed him back, liking where this was heading and wanting more. The next day, he decided to give his brother a call. Wally's wife picked up the phone.

"Hello?"

"Hi, is this Dolly?"

"Yes, Rob, how are you?"

"Fine."

"Wally told me you were in town."

"He told me to give him a call tonight."

"And it's just like him to be at the store. Do you want me to tell him that you called?"

"Sure."

"How about giving me your phone number and I can have him call when he gets back."

"No, there's only one phone and it's better I make the call."

"Whatever you say, Rob."

"Okay, well, nice talking to you Dolly."

"Yes, it has been a long time."

"Talk to you later." With that, Rob hung up the phone.

As he was reconnecting with the family, his girl was heading to work.

Leslie managed to get her nails done, her best frock pressed, and buy a pair of silk stockings, since the ones she was wearing had a run in them. So, with a notebook in hand she bought at the five and dime, she was ready for work. The temp job was in the Hanna Building on Euclid Avenue across from the theaters. She ignored the whistle a guy gave her as she stepped off the streetcar and entered the building with at least ten other people. She almost managed to control her nerves; after all, she hadn't done anything like this in over three years. Leslie missed the first elevator, but one of the operators pointed her to the one at the other end. As she entered, a man, tall, dark, and handsome type in a tailored suit she pegged for thirty, entered as well.

"Hi Mr. Wilcox," the operator greeted him.

"Hi Jacob, looks like it's going to be a busy day."

"I know that's right," he quickly turns to Leslie, "What floor, miss?"

"Sixteen please."

"Working for David Sussman?" Mr. Wilcox said to her out of the blue.

"Yes, do you know him?" She asked as the door opened to her floor.

"A little, he has a pretty good operation. Replacing the girl who just quit?"

"I don't think so, I'm a temp."

"It's just as well." The guy was making Leslie wonder.

"Sixteen, Miss."

"Oh, thank you very much."

"Goodbye," Mr. Wilcox said as the door closed while she walked down the hall. She entered the door for H. Sussman and Co. Inside was a large room with two windows overlooking Euclid Avenue. Besides an office boy was a middle-aged lady who Leslie assumed was Mr. Sussman's secretary and his own office right behind her. The Secretary was on the phone.

"Yes, Mr. Sussman will be expecting you at one. I will

let him know." She hung up and smiled at the new girl.

"Good morning, I'm the typist."

"Hello, I'm Mrs. Sloan, nice to meet you."

"Nice to meet you, too."

"Yes."

The Secretary pressed a button. "Mr. Sussman is expecting you." The door opened and Leslie entered. Mr. Sussman, a short, thin man in his forties with a brown mustache and a receding hairline, shook her hand. "They told me you can type 72 words a minute with no mistakes."

"That's right."

"Excellent, I have this project for you to do." He picked up a stack of paper and handed it to her. "As you can see, I wrote revisions in the margins, so if you can retype it all for me, that would be wonderful." The phone on his desk rang.

"Okay, where, sir?"

"Oh, your desk is over there," they walked back into the outer room,nd, sure enough, on a desk next to the window was a typewriter for her to sit at. Within minutes, she was typing up a storm. As she began her career as a temporary typist, Rob was waiting for his brother to pull up in his cop car at eleven to take him to lunch.

He knew what that meant—interrogation over burgers and pop somewhere—but it had to be done because his brother won't let up. Sure enough, Wally took him to a diner he knew on the West Side. After the earful he heard in the car, Rob wound up ordering the most expensive thing on the menu and a few things to bring home with him to boot. For once, his big brother didn't seem to mind getting the upcoming bill.

"Where you plan to go, Rob?" Wally asked as he finished his lunch.

"West Coast."

"You ran out of dough, didn't you?"

"We have enough."

"So, you didn't like the Big Apple?"

"It was okay. How's Dolly?" Rob wanted to change the subject.

"Fine, you talked to her last night." His brother took a sip of his coffee. "Now, how much trouble are you in?"

"Who said I was?"

"You don't have to, bro."

"Look, things just didn't pan out, that's all."

"Uh-huh." The waitress came over to them with a smile and the extra piece of apple pie Rob ordered. Wally got his little brother back at the dump he was staying at just a minute before his lunch hour ended.

"Been with her long?" Wally asked.

Rob kept looking out the window. "You mean Leslie?"

"Are there others?"

73

He turned around. "She's my girl Wally."

"That's obvious, or else she wouldn't be here with you."

Rob opens the door and gets out. "Thanks for lunch."

"Give Pop a call."

"Sure."

"Hey, don't forget your pie."

Rob grabbed it from his brother and ran into the building. A moment later, his brother drove off. When he got back to the station, Wally decided to pick up the phone and call a police detective he knew in Brooklyn to see what he knew about some recent crimes in New York City. The Kozak homestead was off of East 49th St, and the smoke of the nearby steel mills permeated the air. It was just a two story wooden framed house with a front porch, a well tended yard, and a drive on the side—just like the other houses on the street.

Rob's father, a widower, worked in the steel mills in the flats. They cut back hours, but he was still employed. Pop also had a drinking problem, but not mean or abusive, just embarrassing to his children. Prohibition didn't seem to slack his thirst, which only became a problem after his wife died in 1923. One man left with five children to raise and even in the good years only earning enough to get by. It was a blessing that, eight years back, his older sister Margot moved in with her son to help out. She wound up being the one her nephews and nieces turned to anyway. Wally was the oldest, then Angie, Robert (AKA Rob) and in some places back East known as Robert Cole, Pauline, and finally, 12 year-old Anna.

There was a brother and a sister who died, as well as their mother, who had tuberculosis.

Of course, children grow up and only the youngest two still lived at home. Wally and his family recently bought that house off of Eddy Road that he told his brother about. As for Angie, she and her husband, a guy they went to school with named Tony Vannic, rented a place near St. Vitus's Church and were expecting their first child.

As for the cousin, well, Johnny was in the Navy, stationed in the Philippines with a wife he picked up when stationed in San Diego four years ago. The five dollars he sent his mother in the mail each month more than once came in handy in a pinch.

Anna sat on the front porch with the dog when her brothers pulled up. Aunt Margot was so busy washing the windows on the side of the house she didn't hear the police car pull up or her nephews get out of it.

"Say hello to your brother, Anna."

"Hi."

"How's it going Annie?" Rob smiled as his little sister calmed down the barking dog.

"Fine." She didn't know what to say to him.

A woman's accented voice is heard. "Anna, who are you talking to?"

"They're here!" she shouted back.

"Where's Pop?" Rob asked.

"Your father's shift is today." Aunt Margot said as she walked around the corner of the house carrying a pail. When she stopped in front of them, slightly panting from all the work she did, their aunt quickly pulled off the babushka on her head and smiled. "Glad you're home Robbie."

"Maybe we should all go inside." Wally noticed the neighbor peeping her head over her lilac bush. He took the pail from their aunt as she gave Rob a hug as they went inside. They sat around the dining room table with the crisp white linen tablecloth their aunt changed twice a week, unless there was a spill. She served them coffee, some homemade oatmeal cookies, and slices of potica—or nut roll —that she baked the night before. Meanwhile, the garlicky smells wafting from the stove gave a hint of what they were having for supper later.

"I'm sorry I wasn't able to write this past month."

"We know you were busy," their aunt said as she poured Anna a glass of milk.

"I told him not to call you when he arrived because it was to be a surprise," Wally told them, lying badly it seemed.

"You're home, that's all that matters," Aunt Margot told them as she finally sat down. Just then, the door opened and someone entered the side door to the driveway.

"Hello?" it was Pauline's voice.

"Come on in, Pauline," Aunt Margot gets up again and walks into the kitchen. Suddenly, Pauline runs into the dining room. "Oh my God, I can't believe it!"

"Pauline," their aunt interjected since her niece used

God's name in vain.

"You're here." Pauline gave her brother a hug.

"He sure is," Wally smiled as their sister grabbed a chair and sat right next to Rob, making Anna as a result move her chair closer to their aunt's end of the table.

"I got in a few days ago, Wally knew about it." Pauline just turned twenty and was lucky to get a part-time job a few months back as a telephone operator, but the boss just told her that it might be full-time in the near future.

As they talked around the table, she didn't let on that she was starting to get worried about Rob when she read between the lines in his letters back home. The rest of the hour was spent catching up with everything while Rob tried to say as little as possible. Pop was getting a couple more hours again at the mill since things were starting to pick up. Angie was going to have a baby, while Wally's two-year-old boy was talking like a three-year-old, asking plenty of questions. As for Pauline, she got herself another boyfriend; some Irish guy from the West Side. Apparently, they've been going around with each other for five months now.

Rob could tell from a vibe he got that their Aunt wasn't too thrilled one another one wasn't dating a Slovenian. Angie was the only one who did, and from what Rob gathered, Tony was still the same old jackass he thought he was growing up. Anyway, Aunt Margot learned to love Dolly, and he was sure she'd at least be nice to Leslie. Now the question was, would he want to come back here again, let alone bring his girl to meet the folks?

"You will come over for supper Sunday?" his aunt asked Rob as they were leaving, but it sounded more like a command.

"I think we'll still be here."

"We?"

Wally broke in. "He has a lady friend with him."

Judging from the look that flashed across Aunt Margot's face, Rob blurted out, "Separate rooms."

His aunt wasn't buying it. "She is more than welcome." As long as he showed up Sunday, it didn't matter.

"What's her name?" Pauline asked.

"Leslie."

"That's a pretty name," Aunt Margot admitted.

"What time do you want us to be here?"

"The same as always," she replied. That meant to be there promptly at four, and they would eat at five.

As Wally drove him back, Rob looked out the window.

"Do you know a guy named Joe Lombardo?" Wally suddenly asked.

"Why?"

"I think you know why Robbie."

"I knew him in passing."

"Uh-huh." He made a turn onto Superior.

"I didn't kill him, since it looks like you found out."

"I made some calls. So, that's why you're here?"

Rob once again looked out the window, they were getting close to his place. He just knew that this would happen if he stayed here long enough.

"Well?" Wally asked again.

"Yeah."

"Is she involved in this?"

"Leslie has nothing to do with it."

"Good."

"Copper."

"I'm asking as your brother, that's all."

"Bullshit," Rob muttered, but not soft enough for Wally not to hear.

"You might be in some really big trouble, little bro."

Rob sprung his head back in his direction, angry. "Why in the hell do you think I hopped on that goddamn train, Wally?"

"I figured that out when you came out of the arcade. Can you at least admit that you witnessed a crime?"

"I witnessed a murder, off the record."

Wally sighed. "Off the record. Afraid you might get bumped off?"

"Bingo."

"Think about getting a lawyer?"

"No, not until I get the hell out of here."

"They'll find you in Hawaii if they want to." Wally didn't explain what he meant by 'they'; the cops, New York DA's office, or the one who shot Lombardo.

"Can you spot me a fifty?"

"What did I just say?"

"I'm not going back there okay?"

"You are made to order as a suspect, running away with your girl like this."

"At least I'm alive and here arguing with you."

"They have a description going around back there that fits you to a tee."

"What?"

"I made some calls, someone saw you run from the scene of the crime."

"Oh, shit."

"Well, that's one way of putting it." Wally was really starting to get exasperated with his little brother.

"But I didn't have a gun or anything."

"They are looking for a weapon to match the bullets. The cop I know says that they are aware you have no gun registered to you. Of course, that doesn't mean you could just pick up one to do the job."

"I didn't kill the slob, okay?"

"I know you didn't, but you have to prove it to them, and tell them what you know about that night."

"And get bumped off."

"What did he look like?"

"What?"

"The hitman who offed Lombardo."

"He looked like Boris Karloff. Man, nobody has even mentioned seeing the guy?"

"If he's a pro, I'm sure he knows how to cover his tracks—especially with you running 'round."

"I got to get the hell out of here."

"What about your girl?"

Rob couldn't answer. Part of him wanted to get her out of this mess he's in but, after all she had done for him, he couldn't just ditch her and run away again. She deserved better than that, and besides, he was in love with her.

His brother got him back to the present. "I think it's time to get a lawyer, okay?" They were pulling up to the place Rob was staying. Standing in front of the place was Leslie, who just got off the trolley moments before. He got out of the car and gave her a quick kiss.

"You see? I brought him back in one piece," Wally told her, with an effort to smile.

"Did he behave?"

"As much as he could."

"Oh boy," Rob muttered as his girlfriend giggled.

Wally continued, "By the way, our Aunt invited both of you over for dinner Sunday."

"That would be very nice," she replied before Rob could say anything.

"Okay, see you two then." With that, Officer Kozak drove off.

He put his arm around her waist and waved as his brother honked the horn as the car went down the street.

"How did it go?" Rob asked her.

"Fine, so far. It looked like you boys were arguing."

"We always do."

"What time Sunday?"

"Huh?"

"Meeting the family."

"We have to be there by four."

"When is your brother picking us up?"

"We can take a trolley, the house is only a block down." She could tell by the way he spoke that he was in no mood to be in a car with his brother again. He couldn't sleep that night. He just lay there on the bed, staring at the ceiling. He assumed Leslie was sound asleep since she was on her side with her back to him. In fact, she was as much awake as he, but didn't want to let him know that. If she only knew completely what mess he got himself into.

The next morning, as she walked towards the Hanna's main entrance, Leslie wasn't at all aware of the man looking at her from the coffee shop across the street. If she was, she would have wondered what he was jotting down in the notebook in front of him next to his coffee.

With the exception of a heavy set woman in glasses, the three of them were in the same elevator as the day before; Jacob, of course, had no choice in the matter, since that was his job.

"Hello," Mr. Wilcox smiled at her.

"Good morning," Leslie smiled at the elevator operator too.

"It looks like you're going back to work," the man said in an ironic tone that made her wonder.

"Yes."

"Fourth floor," Jacob announced.

"Excuse me please," the lady said as the doors opened on the fourth floor and they moved around in the elevator to let her out. Leslie unintentionally brushed up against him. He smiled at her as the door closed again.

"Sorry," she told them as she moved back to the door.

"No problem. You'll be getting off soon."

She noticed the scent of tall dark and handsome's

cologne—musky, subtle, masculine, and she guessed expensive. Leslie suddenly got the feeling that he was looking her over. All over.

"Sixteenth floor," Jacob announced as it stopped.

"Did anyone tell you that you look like Loretta Young?" Wilcox asked.

"Not twice," was her reply as the door opened. She stepped out and walked down the hall as the elevator closed with Jacob trying to stop his laughter. If she bothered to look back, she would have seen Mr. Wilcox grinning too. Her second day at work seemed to be going like it should until around eleven, when a woman came in.

"Good afternoon Mrs. Sussman," the receptionist said.

"Good afternoon Millie," she replied, all the time looking at Leslie. "Is my husband in?"

"Yes, I'll let him know you're here."

"Don't bother." With that, the wife walked into his office. Leslie stopped typing, knowing by the sinking feeling in her stomach and the sad look on Millie's face what will come next. A few minutes later, Mrs. Sussman walked out of the office without saying goodbye and her husband popping his head out of his door.

"Miss Adams, can you please come in for a moment?"

"Yes, of course." Leslie got up and found Mrs. Sloan giving a sad smile at her, both knowing what to expect in the other room. Mr. Sussman did pay her for the two days, seven dollars and twenty cents total, and had his secretary type up a letter of reference, and let Leslie know that he was putting a nice word for her with the agency.

Back at the room, she sat on the side of the bed and put her purse on her lap, opening it. Inside the lining were the two pieces of jewelry she still had left. One was a white gold ring with a one-carat sapphire. The other was a gold bracelet given by Jack Martin, which she forgot to return with all the other presents when she broke up with him. As she was rushing to leave with Rob on this escapade, her gut told her to bring them along. After all, if they were in San Francisco as they planned, she could always hock them, and the money would give them a start. However, during all the things that happened from the train to now, being stuck in his hometown, she didn't think about them at that moment.

If she pawned them tomorrow, she would have more than enough money for them to go one as planned. She thought about all this as they rested in the palm of her hand. No, Rob wouldn't like it. She helped him enough as is, he would say. Then again, he would wonder why she still had something of Jack's, and then ask her who gave her the ring. Quickly, hearing a noise, she put them back in the purse. By chance, she decided to walk over to the window and look out on the street. To her surprise, Rob was below on the sidewalk with his head in the window of a police car. Three times in three days.

"I will call you later, I promise." Rob told his brother.

"You don't want me to go up with you?"

"No." That's the last thing Rob wanted.

Wally just shook his head. "Call me about nine

tonight. I should be home by then."

"Okay."

With that, Officer Kozak drove off as Rob ran into the building. He had already decided not to let her know that his brother knew.

"Hi," she greeted him as she opened the door.

"Done already?"

"I got canned."

"Why?"

"The boss's wife paid a visit."

"Oh." He sat on the side of the bed, "Did you get paid?"

She nodded her head. "And a letter of recommendation."

"Boy, things aren't going to plan like I thought they would."

"How?"

"I thought we'd be out of here by last night, and now I'm taking you to see the folks this Sunday."

"You don't want them to meet me?"

"That's not it at all, it's just that we're hanging around here too long."

"And someone might be looking for you."

"I didn't say that."

"Come on Rob, if you really felt like you're risking your life by staying here, we would have hitchhiked to California."

"No, not that."

"So, you want to stay here for now?"

"I don't know."

"Well, if we're staying here for a while, I think we should get better rooms."

When she said "rooms" instead of room, he took notice.

"Will there be a bathroom between us?"

"I just don't think it would look good with your folks, okay?"

"You mean my brother."

"I mean all of them. What kind of a girl would they think I am?"

"Hell, I might as well marry you." The way he said those words, exasperated, suddenly made her mad.

"Please, don't do me any favors!" That was another topic they dealt with before.

"I didn't mean it that way." He stood behind her. "If it means anything, I have thought about it. I just want to do it right. Not here. Too broke to even buy you a ring."

"I don't need a ring."

He put his hand on her shoulder. "You deserve better."

Leslie turned around and looked at him. "I've already got it, Rob."

"A guy on the lam?" he blurted out. "Is that what it is?" Things were now falling into place in her mind. He suddenly turned and left the room. She followed.

"Rob," she called after him as he stopped halfway down the stairs.

"Huh?"

"Please be careful."

He grinned at her, "I'll be back around midnight. Love you." With that, he scurried down the stairs. Rob came back before eleven-thirty with ten more bucks in his wallet.

Celebrate Life

by Lin Bincle

I suppose what is so frightening
is the lonely sound of death
its lonely sound, and
its cold and gripping breath

it encloses all about you
it surrounds you in the dark
it often comes so quickly
it seldom leaves a mark

just a cold and lifeless body
of a spirit that's been freed
and those it left behind you
often with hearts that grieve

Lin Bincle, 1978, observing the funeral of Elyria High
School Principal, Charles Miller.

The Charming Puzzle

by Calypso

No, he's not the average Joe,

His tone of voice is very low,

I had to get real real close,

He told me I was a weirdo,

I said, "Yeah sure, but Di-do",

A mad scientist; I took notes,

He's not like regular folks,

He's from a different yolk,

His charm is no joke,

Figuring him out? There's no hope,

I ain't one to give up or give in,

So I told him to let me in,

To my surprise, he dived in,

So, where do I begin?

He made my mind swirl,

I was clutchin' pearls,

His tales were insane,

Some were full of pain,

Some just entertained,

The more he talked, the darker they became,

What did I unchain?

This man's from a different plane,

Sometimes I feel the same,

So, what have I gained?

He turned my spark into a flame,

The man is full of energy,

What's more, I feel a synergy,

What are the odds the gods put two dreamers both in one
spot?

Add in some drama, it only thickens the plot,

Pen fail me not,

I'm only stirring the pot,

I'm sure it happens a lot,

I'm sure he knows what he's got,

That shit can't be taught,

Here's some food for thought,

That fish can't be caught,

His mind is like a rubik's cube,

Only solved by seldom few,

His charisma is off the charts,

A master of a lost art,

A conversationalist with a young heart,

He's also wicked smart,

Though his thoughts jump and dart,

A pinball machine,

Moving faster than you've ever seen,

You have to meet him to know what I mean,

When that day comes, here's a tip,

Hold on to your reigns; get a good grip,

As for me, I plead the fifth,

But, be prepared when you meet Aaron Smith.

Death, Inc. and the Unanticipated Adventures of Winifred Fox

by Benjamin Bisbee

"A compelling narrative fosters an illusion of inevitability." - Daniel Kahneman

One

On a random Tuesday afternoon, on a well-lit stage while playing the devastating 3rd chair oboe in band in an outdated, musty middle school auditorium, in front of all her classmates and teachers, Winifred Fox suddenly and unmistakably died. Had she been aware this happened, she would have likely been an uncertain mixture of amused and embarrassed in the moment, for she was an odd young lady with peculiarly dry sensibilities. But alas, it was swift and immediate; her autopsy later revealing to her grieving mother and step-father that it been caused by a subarachnoid hemorrhage, pheochromocytoma, berry aneurysm—a sadly silent and sudden killer.

"Sounds juicy." Winifred wryly remarked.

Shush. A terrible thing, the loss of a child, and in this case so unexpectedly and very publicly; it would have nearly ruined the band's continued performance had she been 1st or even perhaps 2nd chair, one might suppose. But thankfully, that was not the case.

"Ok, now you're just being mean." Winifred scoffed in a huff.

Again, shush. Just wait here quietly for Daisey, who will be here any moment. No one expected you to die so early, and we're all being asked to be as patient as possible—you especially.

"Um. Sure. But who are you, exactly? And also, where are you?" Winifred annoyingly inquired.

I am the noble Narrator, my impetuous child. I am not meant to be seen or directly addressed. Something you likely didn't know but now do and should hold tight. I am simply a delightful device to craftily carry astonishing stories along in perfected third person. Oh. That's sort of funny. Another unwanted 'third' color-coating your strange little life.

"I don't get the joke. And also, I can tell my own story." Winifred wrongfully declared.

No, no, my sour goat. Goodness. These kinds of stories, your likely short story, cannot be trusted in first person. Can you imagine? Absolutely not. And it doesn't matter if you get the joke; the joke is funny with or without your feelings or acknowledgement. I wish more people understood that about jokes. And, once again, stop speaking directly with me. This is not how any of this works.

Now, where was I? Oh, right.

In perhaps with any other case of sudden pre-teen death syndrome, when these tragic events happen, people rightfully grieve. A cascade of flowers, condolences, and casseroles are exchanged, and then life moves on for everyone, including strange, sad little Winifred Fox, who would be sent straight to her personal afterlife, as her death certificate required.

"I don't think that's how 'death certificates' work." Winifred irritatingly interrupted.

Once again, Daisey will be here soon enough. Her exact role within HR is to explain all of this to you during your extensive orientation and onboarding experiences. My reserved, solitary role is to simply tell your story without constant, conversational interruption. Your likely limited role is to just inhabit your continued story. Too much unwanted conjecture or exposition can ruin a good story, which is something you might have known if you knew any better in the first place, which leads us awkwardly back to my last critical point with you; explaining why these kinds of stories should always be in the capable hands of the Narrator and not in the vexed hands of confused, off-course children.

...

Huh? No? Nothing? Very good then, let's keep moving without any further interruptions. But petulant little Winifred Fox was not your average young lady, as everyone here in the Eternal Queue understood. Which is why there was such a mad scrabble behind the scenes at her unplanned and early demise. It had been several millennia since there had been a Reaper young enough to be concerned about their abilities and interests but still apparently old enough by anyone's ignorant standards to potentially be denied her lineage—or at the very least, given some conceivable choices.

Because as was now before her was a proposed, ill-fitted destiny, just as it had been for her father before her, and his father before him, and his mother before her, and her mother before her, and her father before her, and his father before him, and his mother before him, and so forth for a few dozen more he's and her's and even few nonbinary, gender-queers sprinkled in as history will prove, awaiting their HR Assimilation Specialist.

Winifred sat in the dark, endless hallway, her arms angrily crossed, her dull face producing eye rolls like automobiles on a modern production line impatiently waiting. Before long, Daisey finally arrived in a guarded panic, trying her best to look like she wasn't just panicking.

"Winifred Fox?" she chirped.

"I guess so," Winifred sighed.

"Good. Good. Ok. Good. Just making sure." Daisey nodded, still trying to catch her breath, hoping that repeating herself while simultaneously pretending that there could be someone else in this endless hallway might afford her the time to settle down from her mad race to get here from the offices.

"Is he always like this?" Winifred droned.

"Is who like what?" Daisey asked foolishly.

"The guy. The narrator thing. The one who's writing all the words."

"Oh. Yes. But you should just ignore him." Daisey smiled awkwardly at Winifred. "They are an important part of the Thereafter, Narrators. And, he is yours. You'll get used to the narration; it'll fade into the background for you very quickly, trust you me."

"Ok," Winifred pouted. "I am not 'pouting.' I'm frustrated. And kinda confused. And you're putting words in my mouth," she stated wrongfully, knowing full well she was choosing her own words in this situation.

"Fine then; you're making them sound bad or wrong with your rude narrating," she said, a bit tongue-tied and senselessly.

"See what I mean?" Winifred gestured wildly to Daisey like she'd lost control of her limbs. "This. This is what I'm talking about. Can people see this? Are people reading this right now? Can they see?"

"Yes. And no. Yes, in that they can or are reading this right now or will soon enough, but no; once they pass this part of the narration and move on to other parts of the story, of course, they won't, clearly," Daisey explained well enough for anyone to understand.

"I'm really not a fan of any of this," Winifred whined. "I did not 'whine'." She inappropriately scolded he who should not be acknowledged like we've talked about several times already. "Dear God," she whined again, even whinier than before. "Ok, fine, fine, I'll stop," she finally and smartly conceded.

"Again, it won't take long before you forget he's even narrating. Although, I do admit there is an edgy, unmistaken tone to his work that could be perceived as unique or off-putting," Daisey remarked unremarkably. "Uh-huh. So do your best to try and ignore him because he is only here to help, to graciously extend his expertise."

She flared her nostrils at Winifred, coming close, but still so far away from anything resembling an apology.

"No, I get it," Winifred stated, finally maybe getting it. Albeit unlikely.

"Ok, good. Sorry about that. Very sorry. Let's move on because it is very exciting to meet you, Winifred. Very exciting indeed. It's a big deal that you're even here, given the circumstances," Daisey stated, desperately needing a thesaurus.

"It's nice to meet you too, I guess." Winifred likely lied.

"Ok, so let's get started, shall we? As we try to do with everyone in your situation, hello and welcome to the Thereafter; or what you might think of as the place between Heaven, Hell, Purgatory, or essentially all the places that people know of, or think they know, about where they might hope or ultimately wind-up after they die. In many ways, the Thereafter is essentially the command center of all post-death afterlife destinationing. Here in the Thereafter, we rely on a highly matrixed accounting and synergistic system of geographic, human-centered conveyance monitoring and placement positioning," Daisey said, essentially explaining with far too much business jargon that the Thereafter was in the business of making sure folks got to where they were expected to go after they died.

"Ok," Winifred replied dryly, like she was smelling a skunk, clearly gifted with tremendous wit and conversational skills. "No, but seriously, does he ever stop?" she asked stupidly, as if she was anything more than a pouty cog in a machine she had yet to barely comprehend in the first place.

"Again, Narrators are important. And they honestly are a delight once you get to know them. And yours is... different, but I'm sure great. I promise," Daisey said a bit more slowly and with a few more swallows than necessary. It was easy to feel maybe the littlest bit of sorrow for Winifred Fox because truly, this wasn't her time. The best Reapers were much older, in her Earthly case, with a sense of well-worn humanity under their belts, making the harder part of their jobs a bit easier because they could relate to one's grief or strife; to the frequent panic or dismay a fresh spirit would often display as they learned what their death certificate required of their accompanied walk through the Eternal Queue.

"I have to tell people if they're going to heaven or hell?" Winifred gasped, like she was just arriving to the party.

"No. Um. Wow, we were not ready to cover that yet. But no, not exactly. In most ways, how you direct them or what they're hoping to understand isn't as important as

99

ensuring they make it to their afterlife destination doorway. But this will all be part of your training.

The business of getting people to where they're intended to go isn't complex in design but can get a bit complicated given the human element of it all," Daisey dramatically understated, still mindlessly reciting from memory the ridiculous jargon from her centuries of training.

"So, I'm going to be a skeleton in a black robe with a giant knife thingy pointing people where they're going?" Winifred scoffed, staring down at her soft, rich brown hands, clearly never having been taught what a scythe was in her blissful, ignorant youth.

"No. Goodness. Not at all. We don't do or look like that anymore. Corporate has gotten a lot more relaxed about exhibiting a more business casual look that suits how you want to feel in the workplace," Daisey explained like a corporate suck-up. "In most ways, you can wear whatever you want as long as it's not distracting."

"Ok. Hm. But, so I could wear a robe? Like a cool, fancy dark purple one? And maybe instead of a blade, my stick could have, I don't know, like a glowing star or something?" Winifred questioned, embarrassing anyone within earshot by her terrible taste and child-like sensibilities.

"Oh! Well. Interesting. I suppose, maybe? I mean, again, you can wear anything, within reason. Most human Reapers just go casual and comfortable. Maybe a nice Earthly suit jacket and slacks, comfortable shoes, dark jeans perhaps, as long as there are no rips or stains," Daisey pleaded with Winifred's poor fashion sense.

"Fine. I'll think about it." Winifred pouted, wishing she could look like a cheap medieval fair wizard instead.

"By the way, I prefer to be called Fred. If you're going to keep doing this." She raised her voice, as if it mattered, trying desperately to sound cool while proposing the worst nickname possible.

"Oh, your records didn't indicate that," Daisey called her bluff.

Winifred had much to learn about the Thereafter. Their knowledge base and subsequent filing system was unparalleled by design, keeping track of everything anyone ever did ever no matter what was done, said, seen, heard, or thought. While it seemed to be taking Daisey a bit longer than necessary, soon enough, she'd find Winifred's known and preferred nicknames, and then...

"Oh, well, ok. I do recall from your records that you've asked to be called this many times in recent years. And that your step-father, Steve was often the only one to do so when he remembered, often trying to impress upon you that he was someone you could trust and think was cool. Or so he hoped," Daisey borderline murmured, making it hard to tell exactly what she was even talking about, given how she interrupted the story in the first place.

"Ah yes, because as I recall, you stopped asking people to call you 'Fred' for this very reason. It's well-annotated that you don't really like Steve, truly trust him, or think he's very cool at all."

"Well, that's true. Ugh, fine. But now I'm here, right? And Steve's not. And I'd like to be called Fred," she emphasized, making you wonder if Steve was really the hero of most of her stories, and sad, poor Winifred preferred to villainize him instead because she's cruel and thoughtless. "No, he's mostly a total nerd, and even my mom would say so. But otherwise, he's harmless. He just tries too hard and expects too much," Winifred offered up as if the damage to poor Steve's character wasn't already burnt to a crisp by her prior disparaging comments.

"Well, Fred, let's move on to the matter at hand. The legal team has asked me to offer you a few distinct scenarios before we continue to ensure that you get to make as informed of a decision as possible, ok?" Daisey got back to business, placating poor Winifred's need to feel special.

"Ok," Winifred shrugged because once again, she was a gifted orator who seemed to only want to bless everyone with her clever banter.

"Good. Your first option is an easy one. You can choose to move on in the Eternal Queue yourself, guided by me, of course, to your death certificate's determination. You'd pass over into the next realm, but in doing so, would be unable to return. You couldn't change your mind once you've walked through the door, and it's been locked behind you." Daisey explained what sounded like the smartest option available, almost as if any other weren't as necessary to even hear or explore.

"Where would I be going? Heaven? Not hell, right?"

Winifred asked, forgetting she knew nothing of this place and wasn't even often listening in the first place.

"No. Maybe. Again, I can't tell you. And that's not how any of this works. Also, I don't even exactly know. I didn't even bring your death certificate for this very reason. No one is able to read the ones from Reapers unless you decided to leave for another plane. If this is the choice you make, I'd simply retrieve it, at which point I'd then walk with you down the Eternal Queue where you'll watch some of your life pass before you on the walls until you reach the door you're expected to open and walk through." Daisey made a compelling argument, deeply regretting she'd not thought wiser about having Winifred's certificate in her hand already, considering how much she was already carrying anyway. It was only a piece of paper, after all.

"Ok. What's option two?" Winifred relented, apparently not understanding that option one was more than good enough for her.

"Right. Option two is you give this a shot. You accept your lineage as a Reaper, and you begin your training; knowing that at any point, you could quit and go back to option one. But, with the hope that you understood and appreciated your role as Reaper, and you adapt into your new purpose here at the Thereafter," Daisey explained stupidly.

"Huh. Ok. And option three?" Winifred asked, again, forgetting that option one was truly the very best for everyone involved.

"Oh. There is no option three. Sorry for any confusion. You can go, or you can stay, with the ultimate option that you can always go whenever you wanted. That's understood by Reapers. It doesn't have to be a permanent job, and it rarely is," Daisey explained as if she was talking to a Kindergartener, which, apparently, was a necessary tactic of communication with Winifred. "You're honestly not helping. Please don't make me report you," she threatened hollowly.

"Can't I just go back to my life? Back to 7th grade and my home? Why isn't that an option?" Winifred asked, bringing the mood back down a bit.

"Oh, Fred," Daisey consoled her a bit. "You've been away for several weeks now; your earthly body is gone and buried, I'm afraid. The people you would be supporting on their journey arrive here shortly after their demise, but Reapers take a bit more time to process. And, in your case, we waited even a bit while longer to pull some things together because we didn't know you were coming this early, like I mentioned."

"If you know when people will die, why was I a mystery?" Winifred inquired.

"We don't, sorry if that was unclear. Lots of this will continue to be unclear unless you do want to explore your training and orientation. The short answer is that we don't know who is going to die or when, for the most part. In some ways, even if we were even paying attention, we might only know because of a recent trauma or diagnosis, or in the middle of a lengthy murder, perhaps. But you'd have to be fairly famous or infamous to make it on our radar up here.

We're all very busy. Because tens of thousands die every day here on earth alone," Daisey explained, a bit too much and too soon, perhaps.

"Wait. You keep saying 'earth' like there is more than just earth. I'm going to be helping aliens or whatever to move on?" Winifred asked, deserving an explanation but likely not getting one that she'll understand.

"No. But you are very astute to think that way. You are only supporting humans, however—Earth humans, especially. Wait. Stop. Ok, let me get back to your original question, ok?" Daisey was clearly rattled, perhaps unprepared for trying to work with someone so young as we all anticipated and worried. "We learn about anyone's death when their certificates are manifested in the Thereafter offices. Reapers then receive them and walk people to their next planes here in the Eternal Queue. No matter who you are, no matter the circumstances, there is no 'going back' to your living self, your body, or otherwise. If that is an option for someone—and it happens, of course—you don't show up here. Once you're here, it's time to move into your afterlife, onto the next place on your journey."

"No matter what I decide, will I ever get to know what my death certificate says?" Winifred asked, as if she'd done anything so bad or misguided in her short twelve years that she should even be worried in the first place about anything resembling a negative afterlife.

"No, you can't. That's not how it works. You can't Reaper yourself. No one can. I'm sorry. But your Narrator isn't wrong, while what you think you know about things like

Heaven and Hell or anything else are probably not what people actually experience? I wouldn't let that part of this cloud your decision-making process. Ok?" Daisey explained, finally agreeing with someone smart about something.

"Ok. One more thing. He's not God, right?" Winifred asked in earnest, making everyone laugh heartily at the absurdity of the question.

"No, he's not," Daisey said far too firmly, forgetting to laugh.

"Thank God," Winifred said foolishly, forgetting that she should be thankful for anyone willing to try and make sense of her plight with such a literary command and passion, instead of being blindly grateful to a modernist construct she couldn't begin to fathom in its entirety even if she had the rest of her afterlife to try. What she didn't understand about a proposed supreme being, creator deity, and/or principal object of faith was insurmountable, juxtaposed to what she also didn't understand about narrators; who are also omnipotent, omniscient, omnipresent, and omnibenevolent, had she even bothered to notice.

"I'm sorry?" she insinuated, apparently unsure about how she felt about insulting creations, much like most of her ridiculous reactions today.

"Omnibenevolent is a bit of a stretch given the circumstances," Daisey coughed heavily, making it hard to understand her. "Sure. Ok, anyway, back to the matter at hand, Fred. Which of the two choices are you going to make?" Daisey said for the win, bringing us back home again.

"I have to decide right now?" Winifred bellyached like a sad, boring puppy who seemed to be tiring herself out by chasing her own tail.

"Yes. But keep in mind, option two in many ways is not having to decide about option one for as long as you want," Daisey explained yet again, getting close to exhausting any new way to explain something so simple.

"Ok. Can I talk to my Dad at all? You said he was a Reaper, too. Is that possible if I stay?" Winifred asked one of the smarter questions of the day.

"Yes, actually, you can. You would. He will be part of your training if you choose to stay. You're actually scheduled to take over for him in his former location. Your arrival means we have to shift a few things around because your Dad will now be relocated to a larger region of oversight."

"So, I'm in charge of a specific group of people?"

"No, a geography. In your case a small city, not much unlike the one you came from, but not the actual city you came from. That would present too many conflicts of interest, as you can imagine."

"Sure."

"Your Dad will either be moved to another city, or he might be moved to a much larger city to work with a team of

Reapers in that location. Again, it'll all be covered in the overall training. And he'll be able to inform you personally about what happens to his assignments."

"Ok, that makes it a bit nicer to consider. I would love to see my Dad again. I miss him."

"He missed you too, Fred.

I'm glad you're warming to the idea of becoming a Reaper like him. It's no small feat to take on that mantle."

"Yeah. Wait. Where did the Narrator go?"

"Huh. I'm not sure, actually. But it's a nice change of pace, I suppose."

"Yeah, it total..."

As it now seemed unfortunately certain, Winifred would likely be staying here in the Thereafter, knowing and understanding that any other path wasn't just uncertain but seemingly far more mundane when compared to the potential life as the 167th generational Reaper in her family. Was she emotionally qualified? Oh no, certainly not. Was she experientially qualified? No, but then again, no one truly is in the early stages of this process, one might concede. While everyone openly worried that this might be a mistake or, at the very least, the extreme failing of an increasingly lax executive leadership decision-making process, Winifred was likely about to become the Thereafter's newest and most inexperienced Reaper all the same.

One could only hope she didn't make a mess of this blessed eternal institution, her proud family name, and the ever-respected duty of those who gracefully and tactually support an individual's essential and often chaotic journey to the afterlife. Only time will tell, and in the meantime, only the rest of us could hope and pray.

"I really don't like this," Winifred wryly proclaimed in a dramatic sigh, repeating a phrase we'd all been saying to ourselves since we first received notification that she died early and awkwardly while blowing a deflating C-double-sharp note on the oboe, making a kind of alarming sharp, farting sound while she slid out of her 3rd seat chair and onto the oak stage panels with a thud. Some thought she passed out because she wasn't a very good player and probably over-exerted herself, while others joked she was probably dead. Those jokes turned out to not be very funny to most shortly thereafter when the ambulance arrived to cart her tiny body away to the local morgue.

"You really will get used to it, and I promise to make sure he settles down a bit." Daisey's thinly veiled threats seemed to have no effect on the ruddy, squinched-up face Winifred always seemed to be making, as if she already weren't unremarkably unpleasant enough.

In an endless effort to aggravatingly pretend this wasn't even happening to her in the first place, Winifred asked where she could get some hot chocolate to slurp during her training. Needing absolutely no explanation, she said it was her favorite hot drink and might comfort her while stationed in the Eternal Queue. Something, let it be known, that was first and foremost her utmost duty, rather than cupping her hands around an unsightly mug of earthy bean juice, sweetened by dried grass.

"Slurp? What? Look, we don't have to eat or drink, but I still can, right?" Winifred inquired, thinking that because something is possible, it somehow became a display of assumed dominance over the entire culture of a circumstance at large by demanding it.

"This falls into the category of your requested cloak, I'm afraid. I've put in your request to corporate, and we'll know soon enough if it's been approved," Daisey placated her, smartly using red tape to avoid any continued frivolity on the subject.

"Is that true?" Winifred demanded, for once, smartly listening to the Narrator.

"Yes and no," Daisey said in exasperation, giving far too much side-eye for her own good in a direction that wasn't even close for the record. "But even if it wasn't true, I don't have the elements necessary to make you something to ingest or wear. This is something that corporate must approve one way or another and then research, find and retain a vendor, budget for, and then source. And that doesn't even account for what goes into whatever policies they might attach to these items that some of my counterparts in HR will be responsible for writing and enforcing."

"Ok. Sorry," Winifred said, finally coming to her senses. "I mean, I still want them; I'm just sorry it's all going to be a pain in the ass." She kept talking, doubling down on her foolishness.

"Ok, so let's get back to your education. Does that sound alright?" Daisey asked, likely wondering to herself if she should have been an Earthly elementary school teacher instead, or maybe a dog behaviorist; either of them seemingly like potential cake-walks given this situation.

"I guess. Why haven't I been able to see my Dad yet? I've been waiting for hours," Winifred asked, confusing everyone who could hear her ask.

"You have. Because. Wait. I thought. I mean..." Daisey poorly explained, confused by the question.

"No. I've been with you the whole time, just like when I got here, in this large, dark hallway," Winifred clarified, shedding some light on her general confusion, shedding some light on everyone's potential confusion.

"Oh. Oh, no. Are you still experiencing linear time, Fred? That can't be, right? Oh, no," Daisey reacted, oddly perplexed once again by the much-assumed complications of allowing an underdeveloped child to take on an adult's role in the universe. "It's not her fault, no stop that," she snapped, speaking well below her paygrade.

Daisey rubbed the bridge of her nose with her forefinger and thumb, holding her elbow with her other hand in a dramatic display of weariness at the frustrating reality she found herself anchored by both her own moxie and her fleeting career aspirations. Winifred wasn't just ill-prepared; she wasn't even exhibiting or apparently even experiencing several of the primary proficiencies necessary to perform her role with acumen.

"What is he talking about? What am I not understanding? I didn't see my Dad yet. Was I supposed to? Does that mean something bad? Am I not going to get to?" Winifred still wasn't getting it. "You're right, I'm not." She had this amusing tact for repeating the very thoughts others had about her that would have made her comedically endearing had it not actually just reinforced everyone's baseline belief that she shouldn't even be here in the first place. "Daisey, will you make him stop," she demanded thoughtlessly, displaying for the one-millionth time her inability to adapt to the Thereafter, her duties, and the respect required of the necessary staffing.

"Please. Please just give her a moment. This is really hard for her, and she deserves one shred of this experience without it being narrated so sarcastically."

...

"Did. Did he go away again?"

"I believe so. I'm sorry, I will speak with someone about him, this isn't normal behavior. I'm not sure why he's so upset with you or this assignment. But let's not waste any more time talking about that, ok? I need to explain a few things to you, and I need you to focus."

"Alright. I will. I'm sorry."

"No, dear heart, you have nothing to apologize for; none of this is your fault, I can assure you. You are just the youngest Reaper we've ever had, and in a few ways, it's presenting a few challenges we hadn't anticipated."

"Like what?"

"Well, first, let's start with the concept of time."

"I'm not like most of my friends. I can read a clock. I can handle a fancy watch, I don't just read the numbers like an idiot."

"What? Oh, I'm not sure if I fully understand you, but that's not exactly what I mean. You even talking about wearing a watch is kind of the problem in some ways. Time isn't like that, like how a watch—as you would understand it —showcases or tracks its existence."

"Ok."

"Ok. So, for you, Fred, for your whole Earthly lifetime has essentially been experienced as a straight line, with each day, each hour, each moment strung one right after another like pearls on a necklace. Does that make sense?"

"Yeah, I think so. Time for me is one thing after another, in a row."

"Yes. Exactly. Alright, good. But here, time is different. It's moderately fluid, nonlinear. It can sometimes be experienced in layers, or slower or faster, or even intertwined. Sort of. For the most part, it's highly manipulative and concentric, overlapping in forward or progressive ways as allowed by leadership."

"You lost me."

"Let's go back to the pearl necklace, ok? Here, in the Thereafter, you can experience two pearls at once or three, or you can weave in-between pearls, or just experience them one right after the other like you already know or have experienced."

"Ok. I kind of get that."

"Great. What you're not welcome to do is go backwards or skip pearls outright. You can. And often, it does need to be done, especially in your line of work; but for the most part, you will be expected to experience time progressively, but with the advantages of interconnectivity, branching, and alternative variables that might overlap or be slightly circular in nature."

"You lost me again," Winifred whined incessantly, unable to grasp simple infinity metrology. "Oh God, he's back," she exclaimed, naively assuming he'd ever even left in the first place.

"Ok, we have a bigger problem. I'm not sure if understanding this even matters. You essentially can't actually learn yourself into experiencing nonlinear time, which is the real problem at hand," Daisey thought aloud, stepping away to learn more back at the office.

"What are you talking about? She's right here." Winifred was really struggling here.

"Ok, Fred, I'm back. Sorry, that took a bit of time.

First things first, have you seen your Dad yet?" Daisey asked, fairly confident she already knew the unfortunate answer.

"No. And you never left; what is going on, Daisey? What am I missing?" Winifred felt like she was losing her mind, which would explain so many things.

"Ok. That's what I assumed. And you never saw me leave for the offices and then come back?" Daisey seemed to enjoy this oddly mundane investigation as if she or anyone else had any living clue what was happening to poor, sad little Winifred. "Which reminds me, I spoke to them about you, too, and there will likely be a minor review of your behavior," she croaked from her dry, chapped lips, pretending she or Winifred's Dad had some semblance of control over immaterial matters that were none of their business in the first place. "Yeah, we'll see what Control has to say about..."

"Winnie!" Winifred's Dad yelled, seeing his daughter for the first time in many, many years. "Look at how you've grown! My goodness."

"Dad?" Winifred looked a bit shocked but still excited to see her father here in the Thereafter.

"Oh, my sweet baby girl, it's been so long." Roger walked over and hugged his daughter, overjoyed at this untimely reunion.

"Wait. Where did Daisey go? Who's narrating this? They sound so normal," Winifred exclaimed with a bit of confusion in her sing-song voice.

"I have no idea where Daisey is right now. I assumed she told you we'd be meeting soon enough once you got here. Do you like her? I always thought she seemed very nice," Roger asked, looking his daughter in her kind, brown eyes, oddly sad but still so excited to see her.

"Yeah, she seems very nice. I was just talking to her. Like, just and then you appeared, and she disappeared. This must have been what she was talking about. Apparently, I'm not experiencing time right." Winifred explained.

"Oh no, what do you mean, Win?" Roger asked softly.

"Um. So, ha. Part of the problem was that I couldn't even really follow what she was telling me. But apparently, I think of time like one thing after another, like pearls, but I guess around here it's different? You can skip pearls or have two pearls at once?" Winifred recounted.

"Oh, goodness. You still think of time linearly. You're still experiencing time like a clock, like on earth." Roger pulled back, intrigued but concerned.

"Well, so I thought so? But you're here now. Because Daisey said I'd already met with you.
That's what Daisey and my Narrator were discussing before you arrived," Winifred clarified.

"Daisey and your Narrator were talking? To each other?" Roger laughed, a bit confused.

"Yeah, he's really annoying, Dad. Not like yours. Yours is so nice and just telling the story; mine is super different. He's kind of a jerk. Super rude. Daisey was actually just telling him that she'd reported him for his behavior."

"Wow. I've never heard of such a thing. I haven't even thought about my Narrator in a significant way in a long time. I don't think most Reapers do. They just simply do their roles while we do ours," Rodger smartly explained.

"Ha, that has not been my experience at all. Mine is snarky and is always interjecting with long explanations and speeches. He's wild. I want to like him, but I don't think he likes me very much," Winifred lamented.

"Oh, baby girl. I'm so sorry about that. I can inquire, too. Don't you worry. Hopefully, the linear time issue will fade. I'm sure that's hard for you; this place is complex enough without that complication. But you must have a million little questions all the same. It's kind of a big deal that you're here. I don't know if they've explained that to you?"

"They did. They're concerned I'm too young, but they gave me the choice to try being a Reaper if I wanted. So, here I am." Winifred smiled beautifully and proudly.

"Aw, that's nice, thank you."

"For what?" Roger asked.

"For calling me beautiful. Sorry. Not you, your Narrator."

"She did? Oh, I suppose so, sure. I'm not sure I noticed that part, sorry. You, of course, are a very beautiful girl, my love. But you don't need to interact with them, the Narrators. You know that, right? Their job is just to develop the narrative as a compliment to your work. Nothing more," Roger explained perfectly.

"Oh. Ok. I'll try not to. He really is kind of a jerk, though. Not like yours. But I'll try and stop. Maybe that'll make him stop, too."

"Most likely. So, where do you want to start? What questions do you have?"

"Huh. Well, first of all, I really missed you, Dad. Like, really missed you. I was sad for an awfully long time. Mom was, too.

Even if she remarried years later to a guy from her work named Steve. He's ok.
A bit of a dud. He's no you. Did you know any of this? Do you get to watch us from up here?" Winifred asked.

"Oh, well, in some ways, yes; in most ways, no. I do know a bit of what happens, yes, but I'm not actively watching you or anything like that, no. It's kind of complicated. And once you're here, your feelings and need to want to know or feel things like that kind of fade. In a good way. Which probably sounds terrible, but it is helpful." Roger smiled softly.

"What do you mean?" Winifred exclaimed.

"In our line of work, it's better if we don't feel too much. Too sad or too angry or too upset, those sorts of things. It would make our job a lot harder because the people who arrive here, the ones we must take to the afterlife, are often all sorts of emotional, as you can imagine. We need to be a bit pulled together by comparison." Roger looked at his daughter with a glint in his eyes. "I'm very proud you're here. I'm so sorry you passed so soon, Win, but I'm so pleased you've chosen to be a Reaper. You're going to make an amazing one and make us all proud."

"Thanks, dad." Winifred hugged her father again, harder this time. "Aw, I am hugging harder, that's true."

"What?" her Dad asked, confused.

"Nothing. Nevermind. Sorry for confusing you." Winifred apologized.

She stared at Daisey blankly, looking deliciously foolish in her wildly inappropriate deep aubergine hooded cloak and wooden staff with a preposterous glowing star atop. Daisey was dumbfounded, unsure why Winifred kept zoning out, nor even thanking her for this abomination of a costume approval.

"Fred? Did you hear me?" Daisey asked for the fourteenth time.

"I was just talking to my Dad," Winifred said slowly, like her brain functioned or how a turtle likely swam through peanut butter. "Oh, so you're both back," she asked dryly as if anyone had any clue what on earth she was referencing.

"Did you experience time-shifting again?" Daisey inquired, about to present the most absurd solution corporate could manufacture.

"I think so, yeah," Winifred whined like a child who just dropped her ice cream on the hot summer sidewalk.

"Ok, so here is the plan," Daisey began to explain, angling for brownie points with her bosses. "We're giving you an earth watch. Like you mentioned, you could read before, with hands and everything.
Apparently, you're not the first person to have spatial-time-differential-disorder here in the Thereafter. But this means you're going to have to exclusively experience linear time from here on out, I'm afraid, or until we can make time for you to try and acclimate again."

"That sounds awesome, actually." Winifred surprised no one.

"Ok, good, this should actually fix things for you, or at the very least, help you make more sense of this place. But it comes with some side-effects," Daisey understated, handing Winifred her ugly watch.

"Oh, no. Like what?" Winifred half-listened while she examined the watch with a scrunched-up, disgusted face like the thing was oozing blood or smell like farts. "No, it's not that. This is a man's watch. Like an old-time watch, and it's kind of big," she explained like someone actually cared in the first place.

"Well, it's the watch corporate sent down. But you

have your purple cloak. You have your staff—with a real star, I might add. That's fun." Daisey pretended to care.

"Yeah, the cloak is amazing. It's perfect. But what you mean a real star? What does that mean? Like a star in the sky?" Winifred asked, looking a gift horse in the mouth.

"In the sky? Oh, you mean like as seen from earth. Yes, of course. You said you wanted it with a star, so we put a star on there, per your request. Do you not like it?" Daisey explained simple things the best she could to a simple child.

"Oh. I didn't mean. Wow. Ok, sorry. No, it's cool. Unbelievable cool. Does it do anything?" Winifred asked, clearly ignoring its bright light and twinkling nature, disappointed it wasn't doing a little dance or asking her about her day, apparently. "No, not like that. My God. So, I'm stuck with you, apparently? That didn't change while I was gone?" she implied, once again, not understanding the first thing about time.

"It's complicated." Daisey, the HR's pride and joy of the Understatement Department declared, feeling foolish she even tried to demand otherwise. "And they also declined your request for liquids, hot or otherwise." Daisey placed a cherry on top of the sundae of Winifred's displeasure.

"I can't have hot chocolate?" Winifred was almost inaudible, her whine becoming a kind of kind of dog-whistle anymore.

"I'm afraid not. Between your age and disorders and frustrations, it's best if we don't give you too many earthy requests, it's been determined. It's all too disorienting and regressive." Daisey offered Winifred another fresh sundae up to her bloating belly.

"Fine," Winifred piously pouted. "I don't know what that first part means, but I am unhappy yes, you got that right. I'm pouting. This sucks."

"I'm sorry, Fred," Daisey wasted her time saying.

"No. It's actually fine because I've finally decided I'm not going anywhere. I'm going to stay a Reaper. I'm going to attend orientation. I'm going to wear this robe and hold this super-weird-but-super-cool-real-star staff and even wear this ridiculous men's watch," she blathered on, bordering on nonsense. "And you're going to narrate me the entire time. All of it. Even if you hate it. I can take it. It's your job anyway, right? So, you do your job, and I'll do my job, and we'll see who outlasts who at the end of all of this, I guess," Winifred proclaimed, not knowing how foolish she truly sounded.

"Foolish or not, I'm going to say what I'm going to say and do what I'm going to do, and you just do your part. Sound good?" She spoke with an unappreciated tone, but one that essentially served its purpose and made its point.

"My goodness, you two are something else," Daisey said, forgetting this wasn't even about her in the first place.

Deathbed

by Lin Bincle

in, out
in, out
white room
black blood
gray face
cold hand.

lights low
eyes back
odd, smell.
Swollen
sweating
dying.

mom first.
Wife, sons,
daughter.
sister,
nephew,
nieces.

nurses
needles
Needless?
tubes in
tubes out
painful?

Tears shed; much Said.
held hand, Touch head.
not near, mike dear.

too young, too old.
too fast, too slow.
what for? say prayer.

roger:
good man; winston, liquor, loved him.
love him. he's gone…

{ Lin Bincle, 1990, from waiting room and bedside of Uncle Roger }

Giving Voice

by Ken Rogers

They had driven nearly two hours—Clarence Furrows and his son, Andrew, and neither had spoken to the other. Long silences between them were not unusual, and Andrew was clearly tired from the long talks he'd had over the past summer, conversations not only with Clarence but with Andrew's mother, aunts and uncles, grandparents, the college admissions office, and, of course, Andrew's parole officer. As the Camry (cleverly packed by Andrew's mother with everything needed for his return to college) backed out of the driveway that morning, Andrew had inserted his earbuds, opened a pack of chewing gum, and focused on his phone's tiny screen. Clarence raised no objection, tuning the vehicle's satellite radio to a smooth jazz station he'd recently discovered, the music's rhythms filling the interior of the car as they passed the mile markers in mutual silence.

"Dad?" Andrew's question was the first word he'd spoken since the trip started.

"Yeah?"

"Can I get some gum? I think there's vending machines at the rest stop coming up."

Clarence grunted. "Thought you bought enough for the trip last night?"

Andrew held a wad of empty wrappers up to his father. "Went through it all already."

Clarence shook his head. "Poor planning, again." They approached the rest area, and Clarence flicked the turn signal. "Make it quick."

"Can I have some money?" Andrew asked as his father angled the car between two faded white lines of the long single-lane lot. Clarence nodded with a frown as he pointed at the coin console between their seats. He then watched Andrew, a baseball cap worn backwards on his head, walk slowly towards the vending area, staring into his phone.

Feeling an ache in his back, Clarence exited the car and walked around the perimeter of their parking space, stopping along the passenger side and letting his rear rest on the front fender. The lead pharmacist of the largest drug store in his suburb, Clarence scratched a belly that—after decades of benign neglect—had finally begun to bulge.

It was one of many physical signs he was entering middle age—thinning hair, recurring back and leg aches, a new set of eyeglasses with more powerful lenses. He looked down at his clothes: faded polo shirt, shorts fraying at the cuffs, shoes wearing at the heels. Even his socks, losing their elasticity and bundling at his ankles, looked as worn as his body felt.

He felt his phone vibrate in its belt holster. Clarence retrieved the device and looked at its glass screen. A text message from Philip Osterman: *Can I call you?* "Jesus, Philip," Clarence muttered as he unlocked the phone and sent a reply: *Not now. We can talk when I see you tonight.*

Andrew approached a few minutes later, the young man glaring down at his phone as if he had plotted a path back to the Camry on the device's GPS and was following its directions. Clarence noticed his son's slender frame, how his t-shirt and cargo pants hung loosely on his body like curtains. "You look good," he said, lifting his chin towards his son. Andrew continued forward.

Clarence called to him again, and Andrew looked up. "Huh?" Clarence frowned, pushing off the Camry's fender from his butt. "Let's get going."

They continued the journey in silence, save for the radio's soft melodies and the muted beat from Andrew's earbuds. Clarence was about to ask about stopping for lunch when the radio signal cut out for an incoming call to Clarence's phone. Andrew looked at the caller identification displayed on the car's dashboard. "Philip? Isn't he the guy we had dinner with—"

"When I dropped you off last year, yes," Clarence replied, declining to answer the call.

"I thought he was cool. His pharmacy's near the school, right? Maybe he could meet us for dinner again after we move in?"

Clarence shook his head. "I need to be at the store early tomorrow, so I just want a quick dinner after we're done, and get back home early. I'll catch up with Philip some other time."

"All right." Andrew took out his earbuds. "Hey, I've been meaning to ask you something, Dad."

Clarence widened his eyes. "What's that?"

"I've been thinking lately about the day you and Mom picked me up last spring, after... my arrest. I was really worried, expecting you'd both be all mad at me. You and Mom have tempers, you've had some nasty fights. But when you saw me after posting bail, you were both so quiet. I could tell you were angry, but it was like you were intentionally simmering, not letting yourselves boil over."

"A pretty accurate assessment."

"Last night, I asked Mom about that day, and she said her holding back had to do with seeing how sorry I was for what I did. I asked if that was also the reason you held back. She smiled and said she thought you had a different motivation, but it'd be better if I heard about it from you. So, since we still got a way to go, I thought it was time to ask about that day last spring, and what was going through your mind when you bailed me out."

Tightening his grip on the steering wheel, Clarence laughed. "I actually wanted to let you spend a couple days in jail before posting your bail. To make sure you felt how much you hurt us." His right hand drifted up and waved towards the windshield. "But somewhere around here, your mother argued that punishing you—she called it 'giving voice to our anger'—would only make you withdraw. She said the best way to get you focused on rehabilitating yourself was to hold back. I didn't want to believe her; we had another of those nasty fights you mentioned, and the only way I could get her to stop was to cut a deal. I'd keep my anger to myself so long as you worked to make up for what you did, but the second you slipped up, I'd let loose. So that's why you saw me simmering when we bailed you out in the spring, and why I didn't say much to you on the drive back home."

He glanced right, towards his son. "All summer long, while you were saying all the right things, fulfilling your parole obligations, doing what you needed to get reinstated by the college, I only kept silent because you didn't screw up. Know what I mean?"

His son smiled. "Yeah." He raised the buds to his ears again, then paused. "Thanks."

"Sure." Clarence smiled as the muted sounds of his son's music resumed. But a moment later, the corners of his mouth turned down, and his eyes squinted. He turned off the radio, cleared his throat, and called his son's name; it took a second call for Andrew to remove his earbuds. "Yeah?"

"Summer ended when we left the house this morning," Clarence said. "The deal I made with your mother has expired. So now I can tell you how I really feel."

Andrew blinked. "Dad?"

"You could have ruined us, Andrew. Destroyed everything we've built and worked for over the years. How could you do that to us?"

"I made a mistake, Dad. It won't happen again."

"It won't? What the hell makes you so confident?"

"Well, I'm not going to play poker anymore, for one thing."

"You think it's going to be that easy? Course you would. You've had it easy the whole damn summer. All these people telling you what to do—your mother and I, the parole officer, the admissions office."

"I did everything—"

"All you did was jump through hoops, Andrew! Like a trained animal. But now that you're back at college there won't be anybody holding those hoops for you. You need to figure out where to jump, when to go. You think you're ready —"

"You think I *liked* jumping through hoops?" Andrew looked away a moment, then returned his glare at his father. "I felt like I was living in a cage all summer, Dad. Even when the court cleared my record, I felt you watching me the entire time, waiting for me to fail. You want to know if I'm ready to go back? Maybe you should ask yourself if you're ready to give up being my damn warden!"

Clarence kept his focus on the road as Andrew kept glaring at him. "Well then," Clarence said. "At least neither of us is simmering any longer."

Andrew exhaled, the hum of the engine filling the space between him and his father as he sank back into his seat. A moment later, music erupted again from his earbuds, the sound muted as Andrew inserted them and Clarence turned the car's radio back on.

They stopped for lunch a half-hour later, by which time their anger had quelled sufficiently to begin a conversation about professional sports. It had always been a safe topic between them, as both were impressed by the other's knowledge and judgment, and there were enough points of disagreement to keep them both actively engaged. Their conversation continued as they got back into the Camry, Andrew taking his turn behind the wheel, and, with his father's permission, tuning the satellite radio to a contemporary rock station. Clarence let his son have the last word in their discussion (a well-reasoned argument that a football team's use of a first-round pick to draft a quarterback was rarely a wise decision), then stared out the passenger window blankly as they continued their journey.

After stopping for gas and more gum for Andrew, Clarence drove the final stretch to campus. In reinstating Andrew after his arrest for petty larceny the college had refused to offer housing. Fortunately for Andrew, his friend Brian had a furnished apartment available in a building within walking distance of campus, and, with the aid of an extra month's security deposit, Andrew had secured a room. Clarence parked the Camry at the rear of the apartment building, then helped carry Andrew's possessions up to his third-floor apartment.

As Andrew opened the first of his plastic crates, Clarence sat on the bed, his body sinking into the uncovered mattress. He wiped sweat from his forehead. The building had no elevator or air conditioning, and Clarence felt exhausted from all the ascending and descending. He took his phone from his belt holster and glanced at the time— 4:41. Clarence looked around the bedroom.

"This is nice," he said. "A lot quieter than the dorm last year."

Andrew shrugged. "It'll be noisier once Brian gets here."

"When does—" The sound of his ringtone interrupted Clarence's question. He glanced at his phone: *Mary.* He pressed the green icon and held the phone up to his ear.

"Hi."

"Where are you?"

"We're in his room, getting unpacked."

"Oh. So you decided not to call when you arrived like we'd discussed?"

Clarence winced. "Dammit. I forgot."

"How's Andrew?"

Andrew closed a dresser door and turned to his father, who raised a palm towards him. "He's fine. Everything's fine here."

"Is he still not talking to you?"

Clarence smiled. "Oh, we talked all right." He sat up from the bed and stood in front of his son, who was retrieving socks from one of his plastic crates. "Why don't you talk to him?" Without waiting for Mary's answer, he handed the phone to a surprised Andrew, who dropped his socks before taking the phone.

Clarence went into the bathroom he had seen in the hallway. After using the toilet, he found a container on the sink with a pump nozzle crusted with dried soap. He pressed down on the pump and caught a thin drizzle of white with his other hand. There were no towels in the bathroom, so he shook the water from his hands before drying them against his shorts.

When Clarence returned to his son's room, Andrew still had the phone to his ear. "Love you too, Mom." The smack of Mary's lips was audible across the room. Andrew laughed, handing the phone back to his father.

"When will you be home?" Mary asked as soon as Clarence raised the phone to his ear.

Clarence blinked. "Dunno. Haven't even had dinner yet."

"Can you call me when dinner's done? Or text if you don't feel like talking."

"Look, it's going to be late—"

"Just text me. It's not a big deal, I just don't want to worry. That's not asking too much, don't you agree?"

He exhaled, long and slow, then nodded. "All right." And a moment later, ended the call.

Andrew squinted. "Everything OK?"

Clarence slapped the phone back into his holster. "Yeah, we're fine."

Andrew shook his head. "She's been really worried ever since Uncle Harold passed. Wish she'd come down with us today, but it's good she's with Aunt Jess."

He then looked back up at Clarence. "While I was talking to Mom, you got a text. I didn't read it, but I saw it was from Philip."

"*Aye-yi-yi.*" Clarence ran his hands over his scalp, then took out his phone and read the message he'd received.

"You sure everything's all right?"

Clarence shook his head as he holstered the phone. "The thing about being a pharmacist is that you never really get a day off. We're always on call."

"But Philip's not a patient," Andrew replied. "And his store's a lot closer to here than it is to your store. Why'd he be anxious to get in touch with you?"

Clarence tilted his head back and sighed. "We work for the same chain, so we share a lot of problems. He knows I've been doing this a while, which is why he keeps asking for my advice."

"You tell him you were dropping me off today? Is that why he keeps calling?"

"I dunno what ideas get into him." He pointed his thumb towards the street. "Mind if we grab an early dinner? All that moving's got me hungry."

Andrew pointed at the empty bed behind his father. "Thought you wanted to wait for Brian, invite him to eat with us?"

Clarence smirked, clapping his son on the shoulder. "That was your *mother's* idea. And in case you couldn't tell, she's not here right now."

Dinner was brief—a pair of pizza slices for each at a small restaurant Andrew had frequented last year. They engaged in a safe conversation about Andrew's class schedule. The sun was still hot and visible above the late afternoon horizon as they walked back to the apartment building, stopping as they arrived at the Camry parked in the rear lot. Clarence extended his hand. "Guess this is it, then?"

Andrew took his hand. "Yeah. Time to jump through some hoops, soon as I figure out where they are." The young man bit his lower lip. "I shouldn't have yelled at you earlier. You're giving me another chance, even though I don't deserve it. So, I'm going to take advantage of it, and make up for what happened."

Clarence took his hand away and shook his head. "Don't think that way, because there's no bigger bullshit in the world than the idea of redemption. Once something's done, there's no way to reverse it, no way to make up for it." Clarence rubbed his chin. "Think of this year as starting over. Like last year didn't happen."

Andrew squinted a moment as if he didn't understand. "All right," he then replied, extending his hand again a moment before quickly drawing it back. "Can you do me a favor?"

Clarence smirked, then reached into his back pocket for his wallet. "How much you need?"

"No, not that," Andrew replied. "I just want you to be sure to call Mom. She's going through a tough time with Aunt Jess."

Nodding, Clarence assured his son that he'd call before getting on the highway. After one last handshake, Andrew returned to his apartment building as Clarence got back into his Camry. His phone vibrated with an incoming text as soon as he pressed the ignition button. He backed the Camry out of its parking space, then glanced at his dashboard and mumbled a curse. As he drove the car back onto the narrow streets of the rustic campus village, Clarence pressed the green phone icon on the steering wheel.

Philip answered on the first ring. "Where've you been?"

"I was dropping off my son at college, like I told you. I also told you not to call—"

"I'm scared, Clarence."

"I'm twenty minutes away. We can meet at the Applebee's a couple miles from your house. We can get there before the dinner rush starts, get a booth—"

"I hu-hu-hate Applebee's."

"For God's sake, Philip. Where the hell—"

"All right, Applebee's is fu-fu-fine. You said twenty minutes?"

"Twenty." After ending the call, he muttered, "Try to keep it together until then."

When Clarence arrived at the restaurant eighteen minutes later, Philip was rubbing his hands vigorously in the waiting area. He looked thinner than Clarence remembered, and his face had all the color of a flavorless drink. Clarence requested a booth, with Philip adding, "preferably one towards the back, away from other tables." Clarence grunted and said any table would be fine.

"I'm pretty sure nu-nu-nobody followed me here," Philip said after they sat.

"This isn't a damn cop show," Clarence hissed. "We're just two pharmacists, and I'm stopping to have a drink with you on my way back from dropping off my son at college. Nothing suspicious—"

"I can't do this anymore," Philip said, looking around quickly.

Clarence blinked twice. "Can't do what? Fill prescriptions from a licensed doctor? Isn't that your job?" A waitress approached but Clarence waved her away, saying they'd need several minutes before ordering.

"I didn't know..." Philip said when the waitress left. He looked around again, then lowered his voice as he continued. "This is a small town, Clarence. You might get away with more in a wu-wu-wealthy suburb like where you live, but..."

Philip put his elbows on the table and ran his hands back over his forehead. "I did the numbers the other day. You know how many...how many...how many oxycodone pills I've du-du-dispensed this year?"

"Philip—"

"Enough for three pills a day for every man, woman, and child in the fucking county! This... if someone asks what's going on, what the hell do I say?"

"You say you were doing your fucking job," Clarence replied, pointing across the table at Philip. "You logged that you checked the credentials of all the physicians, right?" Philip nodded. "And verifying patient IDs, you're doing that too, right?"

"Yeah yeah, I am," Philip replied, looking down at the table.

"Then what the hell's going on, Philip?"

"Wu-wu-wu...two kids in town died this week—OD'd on oxy. A third kid too, but they say he's gonna make it. I mean, what if the pills they took, they got from me? Doesn't that make me responsible?"

"If they didn't get the pills from you, they'd have gotten them from somewhere else," Clarence replied. "We talked about this, back before you got involved. There's nothing—"

Feeling his phone vibrate in its holster, Clarence frowned and shifted in his seat to retrieve the device. He glanced at the screen, then back up at Philip. "It's my wife. I'll make this quick." He then tapped the screen and brought the phone to his ear. "Hey hon—sorry I forgot to call when I left Andrew."

"Where are you? Don't tell me you're in the car, I can tell you're not on speaker."

Clarence winced. "I'm... at an Applebee's, getting dinner."

"Really? I just talked to Andrew, he said you two ate before you left. He also said you were anxious to get back. It's a little odd to be stopping at an Applebee's if you just had dinner, don't you think?"

Clarence took off his glasses, pinched the bridge of his nose, and sighed. "You remember Philip Osterman, right?" Across the table, Philip's eyes widened, like a student being called out by his teacher.

"Of course I remember Philip! Is he there with you?"

"Why yes, he is." Clarence raised his eyebrows. "Would you like to talk with him?" Philip shook his head but accepted the phone when Clarence handed it over.

"Hu-hu-hi, Mrs. Furrows," Philip spoke into the phone. "Yeah, I'm... fu-fu-fine." He looked up at Clarence, who smiled and circled his index fingers over each other before putting his glasses back on. "Yeah, I was...I cu-cu-called Clarence last week, and when he su-su-said he was coming down, I asked if we cu-cu...you know, catch up."

Philip swallowed and ran his hand over his scalp as he listened to Mary. "I'd like that, yeah. Next time I come up, I'll come to dinner at your hu-hu-house. I think your husband wants his phone back."

Rolling his eyes, Clarence took the phone back and raised it to his ear. "I'll be back on the road—"

"I was going to ask you how Andrew was, but now I'm worried about Philip. Is he having a heart attack?"

"Aw, he's just..." Clarence looked across the table at Philip, who stared down at his hands as he resumed rubbing them. "He needed some advice on handling a difficult doctor. Shop talk. How's Jess?"

"Oh that's right, I need to call her. Andrew said he had a good talk with you on the trip down. I'm glad, Clarence. He needs to know he can be honest with you."

Clarence rubbed the back of his neck as he finally realized why Mary had declined to join them. "Andrew's gonna be fine."

"You really think so?" Her tone was skeptical.

"Yeah," Clarence replied. "He...we made the right decision in not giving voice to our anger towards him. That allowed him to learn a lot about himself this summer."

Mary did not sound convinced, but to her husband's relief she did not question him further. After an exchange of marital pleasantries, Clarence ended the call and placed his phone back in its holster.

"I mean it," Philip said. "I can't take orders from those doctors again. I don't care, they can go to the next town—"

"Which they will," Clarence explained. "I ever tell you about my first job?" Philip shook his head. "My first pharma job, I mean. I worked in a lab for six years after college. Right after my wife had our first kid, I knew I needed a better-paying career, so I took night courses in pharmacology. I was 33 when I finally graduated and started working right away at a county hospital. Made good money, earned a promotion after six months. It was right after that promotion when I noticed this one doctor was prescribing large doses of oxycodone. I followed my instincts and contacted the doctor, who told me he wasn't about to let a junior pharmacist tell him how to treat his patients. I then did what I was trained to do and reported my concerns to internal affairs. The next day, my supervisor comes to my station and asks me to step into his office. You think you know what happened next?"

Philip swallowed. "Nu-nu-not what you expected, I guess."

The waitress returned, but Clarence smiled and said they needed some more time. He then glared across the table. "My super reprimanded me, Philip. Told me I should've talked to him about the issue, let him follow up with the doctor. He said my going to internal affairs was going to create unnecessary headaches for him.

When I told him that wasn't hospital protocol for these matters, he said something I've never forgotten. 'There's two types of people," he said. "Those who can follow rules, and those who can get things done." He then dismissed me, asking me to think about what type of person I could expect him to be in the future.

"That's when I started looking around, Philip. I finally paid attention to what was happening in the emergency room, how the nurses were treating patients, all the 'regular customers.' It's when I realized the hospital was more concerned with managing symptoms than finding cures."

Philip smiled. "Treat 'em and street 'em?"

"Yes. I saw that the hospital was a business, just like any other. And when I was denied a promotion at my next performance review, I realized I'd been making some really lousy business decisions, the most important being where I worked. So, I left the hospital for a job at a chain store. And, when I saw prescriptions coming in from that doctor who I reported, I contacted him again. But I had a different conversation with him this time. I told him I knew what he was up to and that the only way he could operate without being detected by regulators or law enforcement was to be part of a larger network of doctors and pharmacists. I then gave him a choice: he could deal me in, or I would call the cops. Soon after that, I was contacted by one of his 'patients.' That's when I got started."

"How... hu-hu-how..."

"How long ago was that?" Philip nodded, and Clarence shrugged. "Eight, nine years, I can't remember."

"And you... you... did you ever think about stopping?"

Clarence leaned forward. "We talked about this last year before I brought you in. Once you start, stopping isn't an option. This operation can't let you stop because it works through distribution. If you stop, people like me would have to pick up the slack. You want to risk exposing me?"

"But... bu-bu-but those kids—"

"Those kids were doomed, Philip, you have to see that. This is a nation of drug addicts. Before opioids, it was meth—and crack before that. Don't think you're saving the world by trying to get out, because salvation isn't possible. The only thing you'd be doing by not taking those orders is endangering the rest of us. And yourself. Just ask Ned Levison."

Philip swallowed. "He... had the store downstate that burned down."

"Levinson was part of the network until he got all sanctimonious like you and stopped taking orders from our doctors. So, they found another pharmacist to take their orders. And, two weeks later, Ned wasn't taking orders from anyone."

Clarence leaned over the table. "All those employees are without jobs now, Philip. Levinson's ruined dozens of lives and made zero impact. You sure you want that on your conscience?"

Clarence realized Philip had stopped looking up at

him several minutes ago. "It didn't seem like a big deal when I started," the younger man whispered, still not looking up, his sweaty forehead reflecting the light from over the table.

"Just selling dope to kids, like in college. Earn a few extra bucks to pay off my student loans. But now... I can't stop thinking about those dead kids. Please, please. I have to get out." Philip began crying.

"Jesus, Philip." Clarence looked around quickly, making sure they weren't noticed. "Pull yourself together. I can talk to the doctors, all right? You send me the data you pulled about your oxy scripts and I'll show it to them. I'll even say it was my idea, my way of checking on you. I'll act all concerned, argue it's time to switch pharmacies, stay a step ahead of the law. It'll be my idea, not yours, but you gotta give me a couple weeks. Can you keep yourself from falling apart before then?"

Philip looked up, tears drying on his cheeks. "Thank you."

When the waitress returned once more, Clarence ordered an iced tea; Philip, urged by Clarence, ordered a full meal. Remembering Philip was an avid sailor with his own boat, Clarence asked if he had been out on his family's lake that summer. He was encouraged to see Philip relax as he recalled a long afternoon with his cousins. When the waitress returned with the iced tea, Clarence asked for the check and paid the entire bill. "Two weeks, Philip," he said, rising from the booth. "Everything's going to be fine."

A minute later, Clarence returned to his Camry. He had parked in front of one of the restaurant's windows, and through its narrow blinds, he saw Philip; the booth where they had sat was directly in front of his windshield. Clarence shook his head. He realized the mistake he'd made in bringing Philip into the network, but he wasn't about to compound that mistake by following through on the empty promise he'd just made. Keeping Philip in the network was a risk he'd have to manage going forward.

As he reached to push the car's ignition, his phone vibrated with an incoming text. Clarence reached down and retrieved his phone. Andrew: *Thanks again, Dad.*

He reached down to return the phone to its holster, but then raised it quickly and turned the device off. He wasn't going to let any more messages, any more calls, any more voices keep him from enjoying these next few hours. Dropping the powerless phone onto the passenger seat, Clarence pressed the ignition button and backed the Camry out of the parking space, the innocuous rhythms of smooth jazz flowing over his body like a warm breeze.

— End —

Gotta Be A Lie!

by Louise Francis

It seems rather it was expected,

caught loved ones by surprise.

When death comes and steals away,

loss deeper than inside.

Trying to piece things together,

rationalize the reasons why.

But, it doesn't make no sense;

death, has gotta be a lie!

People send their condolences,

say things will be alright.

Kind words and prayers while cherished,

the comfort only slight.

Bowing head with silent nods,

consoling others while they cry.

But, it doesn't make no sense;

death, has gotta be a lie!

Going about the days,

doing what is expected, what is right.

Struggling immensely,

there's no place for grief to hide.

Bewildered with woe

at what the new normal will look like.

But, it doesn't make no sense;

death, has gotta be a lie!

Hester's Book

by Nancy Rudisill

Chapter One

How could I possibly explain who I am ?" My name is Laura. Married with a family. Working part-time for a small company. But I don't know who I am and I haven't in a while. I am a shell, a skeleton, an empty vessel; and I have been this way since my daughter Jen passed away. Jen is not my only daughter and I should have enough resolve to be a proper mother to my other daughter, Abbey. I love Abbey, but Jen was my first. My little me. Silly to say, but can you have a love affair with your own daughter? She filled me up with the same euphoria as one in love. The only solace I have found is through weekly visits with my psychic, Claire Durgan.

Usually, I have no problem being a psychic. But today, I hate myself for what I am. Because I know what my assistant is going to say as she walks in my office.

"That same woman is here again for another reading."

"Not again," I sigh. I tell my assistant to tell the lady I cannot come to the appointment.

As I am waiting for my appointment, I see the assistant walk towards me. She tells me the appointment has been canceled due to personal reasons.

Although I'm upset at the cancellation, I decide to shop around and soon spot an old book and pick it up. It's so old it's got to be worth money. If not that, certainly it is of historical interest. There is no name on the cover. I open it up. The pages are brittle and the print is in script. I see various spells. There are spells for good harvest, fertility, love, and revenge. And I know I will buy the book because I see a spell that will allow me to speak to my daughter once again.

As soon as I get home, I drop everything except the book. I carry the book to the sofa and lay it across my lap searching for the spell. The awesomeness of its power escapes my mind. Then I see the words I need to say.

"As below, same as above. I ask you that you bring back my love." I repeat it five times as instructed. Then as the book states. I shout loudly.

"I command you!"

Then I hear her.

"Mom, where am I?"

"You passed on, I'm just communicating with you."

"I'm dead."

"It's okay," I tell her.

I thought it would be a nice conversation between the two of us. But all she is doing is shrieking in my ear about being dead and not being able to see her body. She couldn't even remember where she was before I summoned her to me. But I need to send her back now.

I look in the book. There must be a spell to send her back. But I can't find anything. I got on my knees and prayed to undo what had been done. But nothing changed.

Then, I grabbed the book and ran outside, and placed it behind our shed. I couldn't even look at it now. I go back into the house praying I won't hear her. I can't tell you how horrible it was to hear her cries in my ears. The only relief was when I went out of the house. For I knew beyond a doubt she was trapped. I wanted to take my own life because of this. So I told my husband that I was checking myself into a psychiatric hospital and I couldn't go back to that house. When he picked me up from the hospital a month later. We moved into a condo forty miles away.

Chapter Two

I am some sort of entity trapped. I cannot even journey beyond my own house. So now I must endure the pain of seeing my family, whom I cannot communicate with. After a while, I give up. So in the shadows, I stay. Until a moving van comes up a drive and I realize my family is about to move. I watch with remorseful acceptance. Time goes by. Maybe weeks, months, years—I cannot process time anymore. But one day, a moving van comes up the drive and I see that a middle-aged lady with a son about sixteen is moving in. This house that we moved into has a weird energy to it. Sometimes I feel very strange in the house and I have to leave. Most of the time I go in the backyard and sit on the old tire swing. And today is no exception. I sit on the old tire swing and start thinking of all the families that lived here through the years, and the different impressions they may have left here.

I read somewhere that ghosts are impressions stuck in time. It sure feels like someone is stuck here. Then that weird energy feels stronger and I feel a coolness on my face. The swing emits a sad-sounding creak. Then the rope snaps and I fall down hard in the ground. What *is going on in this house*?

There are moments when I feel that cornered feeling in me growing stronger. I want so much to communicate with this boy. But my attempts to gain his attention fails. I am watching him reading a book right now. I miss reading. And it is at this moment that I realize it's my anger that can make me trigger events because the book flies from his hands and the pages start turning. Then, it crashes to the floor. I know now my anger terrifies him. He jumps off the sofa and runs to his room and locks the door. I follow him and stop at the door. The door is locked, but I bet I can make that old doorknob turn and open. Suddenly, I get a flash. But I see it. My old bed. My stuffed animals arranged in some cartoon line-up.

I remember that I was a little girl here. I see myself getting tucked in by my mom and dad. I stop cold in my tracks. I don't want to be this thing that scares people and delights in it.

Chapter Three

The smell of coffee and bacon wakes me. Today is the first day of school and I'm looking forward to it. On my walk to school, I hear someone yelling at me to slow down. I turn to see a boy about my age. I wait for him to catch up. He points to my house.

"I see you are living in the Mackie house. Did you know that they had a daughter who recently died in a car crash? Shame that she was only sixteen."

"What was she like?," I ask.

"Smart, not my crowd."

"Yeah, but you had to notice something."

"I don't get you?"

"Sloppy, swore a lot, bad temper, smoked cigarettes, practicing witch. Weird stuff has been going on in that house."

"Think she is haunting the house?"

"Maybe."

The depression I feel crawls over me a lot. I am looking at my old kitchen and getting more depressed. Their kitchen is dirty and sloppy. This new owner makes me mad to my core with her messy kitchen. Just then, the cupboard files open and the dishes fly out and fall on the floor. And now, a dark-haired woman is in the kitchen.

"John," she calls.

"Weird." She grabs the broom. A short while later, John and my neighbor, Jack, enter.

"John, did you break some dishes?"

"No."

Jack then says he has to go home, but he will be right back. He comes back with this big book that he says he found in our yard behind the shed. He says it has spells of all different kinds. Jack has to leave without much further explanation about the book. I want to look at it with John, but I can see that he has too much homework tonight to mess with it.

Chapter Four

Hester remembered coming to America. Still small enough to be held in her sister's arms. Hester had been born with the eyes of resentment on her. She was the reason their beloved mother died and might have been easier to take if she hadn't been so much younger than the rest of her siblings. So, naturally, the siblings remembered their mother more fondly than the arrival of the little infant that seemed to be the demise of the family. So, she learned to live in the shadows, feeling unloved. Her loneliness fueling a fire. A fire to be important. You may not be able to make yourself loved in someone's eyes. But you could make yourself powerful. So, the feelings of power replaced the love she lacked growing up.

And the power to be important grew. When Hester was ten, she discovered a secret. She could talk to the dead! She remembered coming out of church when she saw the old widow, Mrs. Kaminski, who lost her husband. Father was coming up to her to offer his condolences, when, out of the blue, behind Mrs. Kaminski, she saw him: Mr. Kaminski! He was holding up his shoe shine box, pointing at the bottom of it. *"Look under here,"* he seemed to say to Hester.

"You should look under his shoe shine box Mrs. Kaminski," Hester blurted out.

"What?"

"Mr. Kaminski, he's standing behind you. He's holding up his shoe shine box. There's money inside it to help you out."

"Hester, if that's a joke, apologize," her father snapped.

"I'm sorry."

But the following Sunday, Mrs. Kaminski slipped Hester a note in church saying that she should meet her this Friday at 7 pm. So, she slipped out Friday and walked to Mrs. Kaminski's house. She knocked nervously on the door until Mrs. Kaminski answered it and let her in with a big smile. She then followed her to the dining room. Around the table were four ladies.

"These are my friends, Hester, and they all have lost their husbands. I was hoping you could do a reading. We would pay you money."

"Come on, sit down dear." Mrs. Kaminski pulled out a chair for her. Hester sat down, looking at the women.

"Hester, you were right. I looked under his shoe shine box, and there was money taped inside of it," Mrs. Kaminski said. And at that moment, Hester found how easy it was to do readings.

"My Joseph, what does he have to say?" The lady closest to her asked. Hester looked behind the lady, but she didn't see anyone.

"That he still loves you. But he is at peace."

"Oh, thank goodness. The cancer was very painful."

After that, it was a flurry of questions. Mrs. Kaminski made it clear that Hester was the real deal. Although Hester did not see any of the ladies' deceased spouses, she seemed to be giving them all the right answers, and it was enough once they believed.

Chapter Five

I see John coming home from school and watch him enter the house. He sits down at the table and takes out his history book and starts reading it. I am looking over his shoulder and I am reading too! I am so excited. I haven't read in so long. Another strange thing that has happened to me since I moved in this house is I have developed a sixth sense. I feel this dead girl's presence. I wish with my own eyes I could see her.

But it's too strong to deny that when I sit down today I know she is here. And I am trying to communicate with her by my own thoughts.

"You like to read Jenny."

"I'd like to be your friend."

Chapter Six

My readings are being requested more and more, and I am now charging money for them. I take their money and go back to my house. I give half the money to my father. Then, walk past my family to my room. I was never part of them. I know that now. But it's okay. Better things wait for me. Then, I take out my book and go to my desk and sit and look out the window. Out there, the world awaits me. And it will be because of this book. My gift is so unique. And this book will be unique. I have already begun working on it. My first chapter is about spells. Mind you, I know nothing about spells. But I don't think it really matters. For the mind believes what it wants to believe. That is where the strength of the psychic lies.

I have been saving money doing readings and working as a file clerk. Until I had saved enough money to leave home to live in New York city. The first year was tough as I stayed at flop houses. But it allowed me to save enough money to rent a table like the other street merchants. With some of my savings, I was able to get some cards printed up that said: **Hester, the psychic who can communicate with the other side.** I kept passing those cards. Then, by my second year, I was able to rent a room at a boarding house. And then, the phone started ringing, everyone seemed to want to communicate with the dead. Unfortunately, a lot of my business was a result of the Korean war we recently fought in. Widows and grieving mothers. Soon I was booking private sessions all over the city.

And, as my popularity grows, I have many clients who bestowed on me many fine gifts. I have countless treasures. Everything I could want but love.

Chapter Seven

My name is George, and until I was about ten years old, I thought I was a son of a nobleman. In a mansion full of servants and no mother to speak of. I remember those early days and the occasional face of my father. Usually in his darkened office where I could not see his face clearly. But it was at this age that I found out what my father really was.

He was not a man. But he was a demon! He had the face of a man. But underneath his desk, as I was looking for my dog's ball, I saw his cloven hooves and tail. He looked at my terrified face and smiled.

"This is what happens when you displease your father," he bellowed out at me. *I don't want hooves and a tail.* So, he said I must always please him in order for him to keep his power. I asked him then what his power was, and his face looked sad. But he said that I must always serve him as he requested. And he showed me in my mind's eye what he wanted. What my future looked like, which was to go above the core to the surface of the earth and sacrifice for him. Anything that caused misery on another human was the kind of sacrifice my father wanted.

I have been coming up to the earth's surface for centuries doing my father's bidding. The destruction of hope and dreams. Planting seeds of hate in people. And, for many centuries, I never gave much thought about it. But now, his allegiance no longer satisfied me. One can only have so much gold or beautiful women before one realizes that these things are one-dimensional and such is the happiness they can give you. There were richer things that I longed for. Things that were not of my father. How I longed for a way which I could satisfy him and also a way which I could also be free.

One evening, while taking a stroll, I noticed a spiritual shop that featured tarot card readings, astrology charts, and palm reading. The shop was called Hester's. So, I went in and noticed it was extremely busy. She must be an exceptional reader to be able to afford rent in this area. Then it occurred to me in a flash. That somehow this Hester woman would be my salvation in pleasing my father. I saw him in my shop that day. Thick brown hair. Steel blue eyes and a muscular body. He notices that I am staring, so I put my head down.

"Excuse me." I look up at him.

"Are you Hester, the proprietor of this shop?"

"Yes."

"Hester, I should like to ask you to tea."

He makes me nervous and the receipts I was tallying up fall to the floor. He waits patiently as I organize them back on the counter. *Klutzy Cow.* She disgusts me. But when she looks up, she only notices my smile.

"The shop closes at seven. You may pick me up then."

"I look forward to it, madam."

I leave the shop and the bite of a New York winter is upon me. I walk back to my penthouse apartment and it never fails that I don't enjoy its opulence. I rehearse this evening. First, we will sit in the parlor and have some tea. And we will sit and talk, I will listen to her. *"Speak, speak, tell me more."* And she will go on, and I will enjoy her company so that I ask her to dinner. Wine will be served in the dining room along with dinner. Then, we will sit in the parlor and talk of subjects. Subjects that I never dreamed someone else beside me could grasp. *"And, at last, I have found you. You precious gem."* And she will be shocked at my sincerity. And will never be the wiser of the master plan that I am proposing to my father.

Chapter Eight

I remember the day I went deep in the core of the earth to visit my father and speak of my plan. And as I looked around at his kingdom I wished more than anything else to never be part of it again. But with this plan, we may reach some kind of agreement. One which I might live as a free man. I will not admit to my son that I cannot do what he asks. Certainly not the manipulation of souls. I can only manipulate conscience. But, to take souls for my own—that I cannot. The manipulation of conscience is my power. Where I can get in a person's conscience and have the strongest of holds. I have had kings do my bidding. I have had wars started.

"If it is what you desire, I will let you go," I told him. And at that moment was when I used my power of conscience to make him think I was capable of harnessing souls.

Chapter Nine

I stop over at my sister Bree's. I am sitting at the kitchen table, drinking coffee in vain. But, it must show on my face that something is not right.

"Well, whatever is wrong with you today. You are lucky you don't have a daughter. I'm sure your problems are small in contrast to mine," she says.

"What's wrong?" I feign interest.

"Kylie. She keeps asking about that book from our Aunt Hester. Told me to buy it for her. Please Claire, don't ever give her that book."

My sister knows the story of how Hester was seduced by a demon. A demon who convinced her to write a book that could supposedly trap people's spirits in the after-life.

"It's safe," I lie to her.

My lying has made me nervous and I go upstairs to use the bathroom. I walk by Kylie's room. I can hear her talking on the phone. There is silence for a while as Kylie is listening to whoever is on the other line. Then, I hear her speaking.

"John, he lives in the house where that girl Jen Mackie lived. The one who died in the car accident." *John, who is John? Could he possibly have that book?* I go back downstairs.

"Hey, I couldn't help but overhear Kylie talking on the phone about some young girl who died named Jen Mackie. I think I did a reading for the mom. You don't happen to know where they live, do you?"

"Well, the only reason I know was there was such a big to do for her when she died. There were flowers and stuffed animals on the tree lawn of the house. It's on Sycamore. The yellow house on the left before the stop sign. Why are you asking?"

"I might stop. See how the mom is doing."

"That's a nice gesture. But I know for a fact the family moved."

"I better go," I tell Bree.

I drive looking for the yellow house on Sycamore. It looks like nobody is home. I wait, hoping sooner or later, I will see somebody who lives in that house. About an hour later, a young man leaves the house. I yell to him from the street.

"Are you John?"

"Yes."

"My name is Claire. We need to talk. I'm safe, I promise." He gets closer, giving me the once-over.

"You seem harmless. Let's sit in the backyard."

I follow him to the backyard patio and sit on a wicker chair. He sits across from me. I notice an aura in him. A bright light radiates from him. It's a rarity that I see a person's aura. But I know enough about them to know that this kid is special as white symbolizes protection and purity.

"My name is Claire Durgan. I believe you know my niece, Kylie. She goes to Village Falls High School."

"Yeah, goth chick with long dark hair."

"That's right."

"The reason I am here is I overheard Kylie talking on the phone. She mentioned that you were living in this house now. See, the lady who lived in this house before you had a daughter who died. She was always bothering me for a psychic reading. And I grew tired of her. And I gave her a book that I shouldn't have. A book about summoning the dead."

"Wait a minute." He leaves to go into the house and comes out shortly thereafter.

"This book." *And there it is. Hester's evil book for summoning the dead!*

"You didn't use it," I ask.

"No."

"That's good. Now, I don't claim to have any powers anything near to what is mentioned in that book. But I did keep that book as part of my collection, as it belonged to my Aunt Hester. But as far as I am concerned, that book should have never been used. And nobody did use it. Except in a moment of insanity I gave it to someone who I believe is the mother of a deceased girl named Jen Mackie."

"Oh, my God," he says.

"What?"

"I have been feeling her energy since the day I moved in. We speak to each with our thoughts. The poor thing is scared. Her existence has no meaning to her being trapped in this house. It really is a form of hell."

"I need to have this back." I point to the book.

"Sure."

"I've got to go, but I'll be back."

Chapter Ten

"Would you like to be rich?"

"Huh?" I answer back. Preoccupied by the white cherub pouring water from a jug in the fountain, the flower gardens, and the acres of manicured lawns.

"This is you, not me." He sets my wine glass down.

"It could be you." He takes me into his arms and kisses me passionately. My first passionate kiss! I am in love with this man. And, as they say..."*The rest is history.*" He takes over every aspect of my life. Soon, my customers are swooning over him. They all adore him. As my clients have doubled, maybe even tripled. I make plans to move out of my apartment and into his mansion.

"Will we be married soon?" I ask him on the day I move in. He doesn't answer. Instead, he kisses up my neck and whispers in my ear.

"Let me have that book you have locked up, and I will make you rich and powerful."

He grabs my hand, leading me into the bedroom. His hot love taking over my body and mind like a virus that will never leave. When we are finished, he gets up for a moment. But soon, he is crawling back in bed with me, kissing me all over. I wait for the catch. Things like this don't happen to girls like me. And there it is. He has taken the book.

"Use this, my darling. At your next séance. You should say these words." He shows me a page in my book that he has written on. I read the words then look up from the book confused.

"I'm not really summoning the dead?"

"Of course not, darling. It's just a touch of drama. It will make you different from any other psychic."

"I have everything I need," I tell him in vain.

"One could always use more." His hand quickly moves up my thigh, and I let out a gasp of delight.

George follows me that evening where I am booked to do a séance. He has the book under his arm, as I have agreed to use the chant for the first time. The lady wants to communicate with her daughter who died in her twenties. George lets me proceed the way I usually do. And I ask her questions, hoping for the clues that will give me vague answers disguised as important imparted knowledge.

"Yes, she is at peace. She misses you." And the client seems satisfied enough. Not terribly impressed, but accepting anyway. She is ready to get up and leave when George opens the book. He says we need to hold hands together so we can make stronger contact. The lady decides to sit back down and we all hold hands.

"Say the words, Hester." I say them. At first, my voice is unsure. But then, my voice grows stronger, and I chant loudly until I am finished. Then, I ask, "Millie. Do you hear us?"

"Hello, Mother. How have you been doing?"

I am shocked, because I am listening to a back and forth conversation with a dead person. An actual two-sided conversation! I look over at George just now, and he gives me the most wicked and deceptive smile. It sends a shiver up my spine. "I got to go," Millie announces.

"Okay, darling."

I am waiting for the séance to come to an end. That is where the spirit goes on to the other world. But I can stop this spirit in this world. Thanks to Hester and her chant. Stupid woman. And now, any souls of the deceased who she thinks she has innocently called. They will now be in my grasp and I can offer them to my father. This plan is brilliant for I hardly have to do any work in order for it to happen.

Chapter Eleven

I cannot believe how famous I am. Here I am, doing readings all over the country. Readings where my audience is held captive. The conversations they have with their departed. The words, that book. It's the magic I dreamed about since I was a little girl. And now, it's true! Me and my handsome boyfriend. He follows me everywhere. When I do my readings, when I am invited to talk shows on TV. There he is, sitting along beside me. Charming and witty. He makes the host laugh, the audience laugh, and everyone loves me because he loves me. But I am so plain and he is so beautiful. I need to find a way to hold him to me.

"I want to get married." I tell him one day as we sat down to dinner. But I already know the answer. Nervous, I hold my wine glass to my lips. He wipes his mouth and glares at me. "I have them, you know." And now, it seems I am hearing a thousand voices. All talking at once. Unyielding chatter. I claw at him.

"What have you done?" Then, he grabs my throat,

squeezing it fiercely. "I thank you, but I must bid you adieu," he tells me. Everything becomes black. When I awake, he is standing above me. Along with two ambulance drivers dressed in white.

"I'm afraid she needs to be where she is safe," he says to them. I'm loaded on a gurney. George follows me to the ambulance and kisses my cheek before they take me away.

Chapter Twelve

High above the earth. There was a kingdom. It glittered full of breathtaking light. Every color in the prism shined which resulted in translucent pearly white orbs that were shone upon the earth. The orbs were full of love, protection, and wisdom. And the orbs channeled its energy through the people of the earth. For it was told among the people these beautiful orbs were a gift from the universe. Because the goodness that the people of the earth radiated back to the universe. A famous astrologer from that time had predicted because the people of earth were starting to change their loving ways that the beautiful kingdom of light would soon collapse upon itself. And all that would be left were those who fell from the kingdom of breathtaking light onto the hard earth. And because of this a battle would begin. It was also said that these orbs being sent down were now more important than ever. As the earth was growing dimmer each day. They were needed now to lead as many people away from the darkness as they could.

Those who fell from the glittering kingdom to earth were mad that they were sent down. Forgetting about the ways of love, protection, and wisdom. Unable to forget that they were cast down, they transgressed and defied in their hearts all that was good and right. The fallen ones made a neutral place and cried out to the kingdom they had been cast from to allow this place. A place where dark forces could meet. And at this meeting place one would be allowed to pledge their allegiance for eternity. As most of them never got over being angry for having been cast down and had aligned themselves to the darkness.

Chapter Thirteen

I put my Aunt Hester's book in my trunk. I decided to close the shop early because I am too nervous to work. I grab a bottle of wine and some crackers and go to my bedroom and put the book on the bed. I open the book to where the chant is. It's shameful to admit that I never really thought in-depth about the chant. I wish I did before I let that lady wear me down enough to give her the book. But, my search for answers is denied—and the only comfort that exists seems to be found in the bottom of my bottle of wine. Soon, I am drunk, and crawl under the sheets. No better than I was before. I fall into a deep sleep. But, like a miracle, I'm being downloaded with the answers to the questions I am asking. I'm being told that John is a protector of sorts. Protecting those who cannot protect themselves. He is interceding on this girl's behalf. He is a prophet of light, here to restore the balance of light and dark forces. And, when I awake, everything is crystal-clear about John and his purpose. The only thing I don't know about is the dark.

Chapter Fourteen

The weight of what I have done resides with me each time I rise at the state mental hospital in New York. To them, I am just another delusional person. But my delusions are real. So, I try to run away from myself, what I did, what I've become. Most of the time, I am kept in seclusion away from the other patients. The days here are empty and painful as everyday I'm reminded how pure evil disguised itself as love in my life.

The ocean air assaults my nostrils, and I feel a breeze upon my face as I wake up. It is a delightful way to wake up. In fact, I have woken up like this for the last thirty years. Usually, with a beautiful woman in my bed. And I feel good. My father has freed me of my burden. I am a regular human. There are days that I wish I wasn't. Now that my hair has turned white and my bones ache when it rains. But I look out at the ocean and in a few moments, I forget what I have given up. On my deck with my little dog beside me hearing the waves. A woman coming out of the kitchen giving me a cup of coffee and sitting on my lap while I caress her back. Is she the one I will grow old with and hold my hand when I die?

I think upon my old life through the centuries. The pain and hurt I have caused. And my most recent hurt, Hester. And, as I have become mortal, I feel the waves of guilt because of what I have done to her. Perhaps that is why I like the ocean so much. That like my guilt every wave that washes upon the shore will reside eventually.

Chapter Fifteen

It's Saturday morning, and I'm sitting on the front porch when I see a familiar looking car creep slowly in front of my house. I recognize the lady in the car. The lady who has my book. That psychic woman, Claire.

"Hey," she flags me over with her hand, and I walk up to the car.

"Can I help you?"

"We need to talk. Get in the car."

I hop in her car. As we drive along, a crystal pendulum swings from the rearview mirror and emits a tiny laster show.

"Okay, I'm in your car. Can you please tell me what is so damn important?"

"You are chosen." She turns, looking dead on at me.

"Please, look at the road. Chosen for what?"

"You are the one who can speak to her. I was being downloaded in this crazy dream. That the reason that you can sense Jen is because you are a prophet here to help restore balance."

"I don't understand."

"You can hear her and you know damn well that she's trapped. You are also a person who will not use evil to help her. But you are the one. It was all revealed to me in a dream.

I'm a bit psychic. Did you forget that? But you do believe what I'm saying, don't you, John?"

"Believe that I have some great powers that can save people? I just want to save Jen."

Chapter Sixteen

I have a problem. No hot water. I am trying my best to not call Mr. Mackie, my landlord, who has not been exactly been the most approachable person towards me. So, I have a friend looking at it.

"Can you fix it?" I ask.

"It's definitely not working. Better call the landlord."

"Well, I appreciate you looking at it." I walk him to the door. Then, grab my phone to call the Mackie family. The phone rings a bit then finally someone picks it up.

"Hello?"

"Hello, is this Mr.Mackie?" I ask.

"Yes."

"I'm renting your house on Sycamore. My hot water tank is not working." I feel extremely apologetic, although it is his job to fix it.

"Can it wait until tomorrow morning?"

"That will be fine," I tell him.

Chapter Seventeen

I am sorry I released him. I should of refused him. But, I had to let him go. That was the only way he would of loved me. Even the light knows you cannot bend someone to your will. But George is never far from my sight or my heart. Oh, did you think someone from hell does not feel love or regret? Mostly, I feel regret. Here I am, strong—and he is dying. For he is among the mortals. I always thought I knew what was best. But, I see it isn't so. For in trying to please me, he has ruined someone's life. And now, he is on a path trying to right his wrongs.

Today is one of those days when I miss giving up my power. I spent hours on the internet looking up Hester Durgan. She is still at the New York State Mental Hospital. And now, I am on the freeway, driving to see her. All the while enduring honks from other drivers because of the shitty way I drive now. I am an old man near seventy-five. I battle arthritis and have moments of forgetting. But I think I made the right decision by being mortal. I think I will die clean. I think dying means leaving no ties behind. More like big ugly knots. I have a big knot to untie with Hester.

Chapter Eighteen

It's up to you to help him see his gifts. This is the first thought I have this morning as I pour coffee into my cup. John's powers are real. I know that beyond a doubt. That chant that was in my Aunt Hester's book. Is there any way to take the curse off it? Maybe I should try to find Aunt Hester. Maybe she can help John.

I go to the phone and call an old boyfriend, Gary, who I still keep in touch with. He's a private detective who came to me to see if I could help him as a psychic solve a case. He had a good laugh, because the first two leads were bogus and he fired me.

However, later that evening, I was able to connect to a partner on the force that died during his watch. Sometimes, I am for real. Also, after a few drinks that night, I was able to give him another kind of peace. We get together semi-annually for a booty call. Mostly because we're both gross in our own way.

"Claire," he picks up. He sounds happy. Cops are never too far away from needing some form of release. *Sex or drinking.*

"It's not that kind of call," I explain.

"I need you to look up an address. And then I got to go there as quickly as possible."

"Give me a few minutes and I'll call you right back," he says.

Chapter Nineteen

"You have a visitor." I rouse myself out of sleep and sit on the side of the bed and put my slippers on. "Who is it," I ask.

"Someone named George."

Did I hear him right? There is only one George. The one who put me in this hell-hole to rot. Listening to the voices day after day of those who cannot rest. And it is because of me they cannot rest! The orderly walks me into the common area, but I don't see him. Either that, or I don't recognize him. Then, he sits me at a table across from an elderly man. His face is old. But the blue eyes, I recognize them. It's George! And before I can grasp what has happened, I hear a different orderly calling out my name.

"You have another visitor." And the orderly walks a middle-aged woman with long brown hair to the table and sits her across from me next to George.

"She says she is your sister Stella's daughter."

I hardly remember Stella, let alone her daughter. George locked me away in here so young. Locked me away from everyone.

"Hester, I know we have never met, but I am here to give you something back that once belonged to you. Also, I need for you to help me. I think I have done something very bad."

She slides the book to me.The book that so long ago started it all. When I see the book, I feel the rage that built inside of me because of it. I grab the book.

"You did this to me." I throw the book at George. And then, an orderly grabs me from behind. "Visiting hours are over."

Chapter Twenty

I don't recognize this blue-eye elderly gentleman."Who are you," I ask.

"George," he answers simply.

172

He grabs my hand and leads me to some chairs in the hallway where we both sit down. And I notice that he wants to sit not only to talk to me. But he is very old, and is out of breath. But slowly I can see. The eyes. Those piercing blue eyes are still the same. It's just the face that has changed. More lax and wrinkled. But I can see how he could have seduced her.

"How could you have done that to an innocent girl? You ruined her life. That book, that chant. It was your book. You are a very powerful demon. And now you look like an old man. Huffing and puffing when you speak. What could you possibly want with her now?"

"We won't get anything accomplished if you are throwing all these allegations towards me. You know as well as me, Claire, that you can't change the past. You did something wrong, too. Have you not, Claire?"

"The book," he says. He points to my lap. I hold the book shamefully. His piercing blue eyes bore through me so that soon he's got me spilling my confession.

"I might have unwittingly unleashed its power again. I admit I did use Hester's famous name in order to help my business. Might of kept that book in my shop to hypnotize the customers into believing the stories. I might of let myself not believe that the book was cursed in darkness. But her legend had made me immensely popular. And there wasn't really any harm. Until a lady whose daughter died had become obsessed with the stories and legends of Hester and wanted a reading. But she kept on wanting more than I could give her. She wanted me to communicate the way she heard Hester could. I guess I just got so tired of her coming around that I let myself get worn down by her and gave her the book."

I look down at my feet. I feel as irresponsible as a five-year-old kid just now. "I know very much about getting worn down. And what were you supposing Hester could help you with?"

"Well, the mother had used the chant in the book to bring back her daughter. And now, the daughter is stuck between worlds. I thought maybe there is something in the book that I did not notice that might help this girl."

"Hester's powers lie in me." His tone is sharp and agitated.

"How do you know she is stuck? Did the girl's mom tell you?"

"No, the mom freaked out and left the book when she moved. Fortunately though, we got the book back from the person who lives there now. A boy who can communicate with the girl who died. He has a legend of sorts attached to him, too."

"A legend, you say?" George stands up.

"You must tell me all about it on our ride to this boy's house."

Chapter Twenty-One

I hate to admit it. But George's company delights me. He is charming and wise and understated. He tells me his only intention was to come and apologize to Hester. But that can wait. Now, he wants to know about the girl who is stuck between worlds and the boy who can talk to her.

"Is he a demon too?" He rustles a cigarette out of the pack, then fishes for a lighter in his pocket.

"There was a time I could light these with my fingertips."

"Yeah, well your resume is quite impressive from what I gather. How many souls did you gather with that chant anyway?" I look over at him.

"I don't know, I did my father's bidding back then. But I have been banished from him after I gave up my power." He flicks a cigarette out the window shortly after he lit it because he is having a choking fit.

"So, you used the book as sort of an urban legend to boost sales. And now you got caught in a snare. Good things usually have snares attached to them. That is how the light works. The light likes to keep one humble. You know, like the song, "Oh, Lord, it's hard to be humble.""

"You know about the light?" I feel shocked. I thought his whole world was etched in darkness.

"Of course, without light, there is no darkness. You know, the yin and yang thing."

"That makes sense."

"But this boy that can talk to this girl who is stuck between worlds. What makes him so good?"

"You will see. It's hard to describe. But he has this white aura to him. You can tell he is good."

Before I know it, we are off the highway and are driving down endless tree-lined streets. Each lawn more manicured than the other. I think I have found a new version of hell. Bland and predictable. It's hard to believe that this town harbors my adversary. The one who has been able to break through my spell and communicate with a soul I have trapped. After I have set everything in motion. And I feel the fragility that comes with every man who is mortal. That the things we have done are really meaningless. Easily blows away like sand in a windstorm.

Perhaps nobody makes their mark like they think they do. Not even those with great power. And then, I see him. The young man who is good and pure. A white aura is all around him.

"Come on," says Claire.

But my hand stays frozen on the door handle of the car. For this man/boy/child prodigy, whatever he is emits a light that pierces my heart. As if he's holding my heart in his hand. Now, stripped of its barriers. We are man to man, spirit to spirit, soul to soul. No introductions need to be made. For he has already read my most innermost thoughts. I hold my mind steady, holding up the walls I feel crumbling. Hoping that there is a seed he can find and sow from me. That shows him I'm not all bad. Although, I have done countless bad things to Hester and countless others. This girl who he can speak to in this house. And as he comes out, I hear the endless crying and the screaming of all the anguish and terror I have caused. And I realize his powers are much greater than mine have ever been. Even in my strongest of days.

"Oh shit, there she is," I hear Claire say. I'm just getting out of the car. But another distraction is just what I need right now, so I can figure this out.

"Who is that?" I ask Claire.

"That's the one I gave the book to. It's the girl's mom. The one who used the chant." Following her is a man I assume is her husband, along with their kid, who looks about fourteen years old.

"I could kill you," the mom runs up to Claire. All of a sudden, the mom puts her hands over her ears.

"It's Jen. I can hear her crying out to me. How could you let me do something so evil?" She kneels on the ground now, writhing her body back and forth.

"Please, release her. She's trapped," Claire yells out to John. By then, John, whose light is brighter than ever, walks over. He holds his hand out to her and gently helps her up.

"I can't help you," he says to her.

"Only he can." And he points to me.

"Give me the book."I grab the book from Claire and begin to flip through the pages.

"It doesn't work that way. You gave up your powers a long time ago, George."

"But this lady is suffering."

"Then you make it stop," I tell him.

"I can't without you. But I need a sacrifice. One so big it should surpass all other sacrifices done. And his voice changes to my father's.

And I remember thinking in my head those same thoughts. *A sacrifice so big, I shall no longer have to do my father's bidding.*

"And what exactly is that sacrifice?" I ask him.

"It's you. You have three hours.I will be back then if you wish to surrender yourself to me."

I look at him like a wounded dog. If I had not given up my powers I would of ripped through him. But, here I am—stuck like a punished child. I go to the house and sit on the front steps.

"Hello," a girl's voice echoes in my ears.

"Can't you help me?"

She is crying in my ears. So loud I can't think. I curse myself. Why did I ever develop a conscience? Should of never concerned myself with Hester's forgiveness. I could still be sitting at my beach house watching the waves. Why did I care about these people who are so much lower than me? But I did. And now, I'm stuck here, with the whole stinking rotting mess. Them, who never showed me much love or joy. I had found far more joy and love before them. But yet, I am bound to them. A circle of imperfection. I have muddied my hands of them, and now I can't wash it out. There will be no peace until I take care of them. I must surrender myself, for that is the only way to live.

Three hours go by, and I am still on the porch. I have

nowhere to go but home. But so shall I live with myself then. Jen has mercifully silenced herself from my ears and I know my time is about up when John, the light, comes up the driveway. Everyone else he commands to stay in the car. He walks up slowly and I am reminded of those old westerns I've seen on TV. The stand-off.

"Well, have you decided?" he asks. I look out at the driveway. Prying faces are stuck to the window.

"What's to become of me?" I ask.

"I cannot answer that."

"Shall I be no more?" I ask.

"Your decision is now."

"Then I will go with you," I tell him.

He places his hands on my head. When I open my eyes I am on a long bridge. Thousands and thousands of feet are below me.

"Where am I?"

"*The Bridge of all Creation.*" I walk toward a bright light. Behind me is a tunnel of darkness.

"Do I have a choice?" *Then he tells me that love is love and the only hell is the one you make in your own mind.*

"So, those souls with Hester, were they not trapped?"

"*They were never trapped, but you were. And Hester was, too. They were in your conscience as the consequences of your actions.*"

"What about Jen?"

"She was given a purpose by me to bring John to her. John to Hester and her book. And Hester and her book to you. And you to me. Now, we are a circle unified. Don't you see you put yourself in hell, your own conscience? But then, you were remorseful, and longed for forgiveness and showed humility. That is all we really can do as spiritual beings. But if you knew you were protected, what would you have learned? I am creator of all. Good and bad. And they work in ways you can't understand. Even your father was my creation. But if things are given to you, you won't learn. I have given you free reign, free will, whatever you want to call it. But there is always a reason for anyone's pain and tears.

"What is that?"

"That I am still in your heart. Letting you know that I still love you."

Kringelein Account

by James Valentino

The house was on a nice street with residences in a medley of styles; some of them quite large, within walking distance of the Boston Mills Country Club. Built in 1940, it was a higher-end Cape Cod with a lot more going for it than merely two white dormers on the second floor. With an attached garage, slate roof, a nice front yard that sloped to the street with plenty of grass to mow, even a gazebo in the back, it was picture perfect to anyone driving by.

It wasn't Dan Wyatt's intention to buy this place, but having driven past it so many times over the years, he always mused about what it would be like to live in it. When it came on the market for $325,000 in March, after returning from his trip to Costa Rica, he took the leap and emailed the realtor. Within a week, they accepted his offer of ten percent down and called up the movers. The Savings and Loan would only give him a 15-year mortgage due to his age, but that didn't matter. He knew he wouldn't be around in 15—let alone 30 years—to pay it off.

Being handy himself and possessing little in things to bring from his apartment, Dan had no trouble getting the place in order by the end of June. Right now, as Dan looked around the rooms, it appeared like he was living there for years. When he closed his front door to take a jog, he couldn't help but look back and admire the place he now called home. To him, this was heaven.

He took up jogging about a year ago, right after Ralphie died. Never a great runner growing up, he could still get out of breath halfway through, but nowadays, Dan could keep up for at least half an hour. It helps to be able to run around these streets with the pretty houses; well-kept lawns, and trim shrubs, as he puffed for air. It sure was something he wouldn't want to do around the area his old one-bedroom studio apartment was located. He saw someone using a weed whacker in front of a Tudor-style mansion to his right; the one with all the red and white azaleas blooming in May.

"Hi," he greeted the man who merely waved back and continued to trim his sidewalk. The weatherman said it was going to be 73 degrees for a high and, looking up at the blue skies and feeling the small warm breeze from the south, Dan was glad he was finally right. It will be a nice birthday after all.

A car let him go across the street at the stop sign as he continued on his journey around his neighborhood. He turned 70 today, and he had all the curly gray hair to prove it.

A tall, skinny man, Dan lived in this town all his life. It seemed that the past 45 years of his life all he did was work; half the money going to pay down the student loans, and after that, to pay off the expenses that went into his mother's care the last years of her life.

To think he was still working at that dead-end job only a year ago when, suddenly, on his last birthday, he told his boss, a woman half his age he trained when she first got hired over a decade ago, that he was retiring ASAP. So he took out all his money in the 401K and cashed in one of his life insurance policies—the $50,000 one that matured. He even sold his little pile of stocks, the "Kringelein Account" as he called it, referring to the Lionel Barrymore character in

the movie "Grand Hotel."

It may not be enough to live on for 30 years but after all, didn't they set retirement age for Social Security at 65 back in the thirties because most people dropped dead in the meantime? So, what the hell—you only live once as everybody said. As it turned out, Dan did more in the past year than he had done in the previous forty.

Suddenly, the fast pace of his jog caught up with him, and he had to stop. There he was, in front of a white French Provincial, with a picture-perfect green lawn, bent over to catch his breath. The white boxy mail truck was coming up the road on its daily route. Getting back up, Dan walked across the brick street so he could get out of its way. After all, the mailman probably just got done delivering his mail back at the house.

When he got home, Dan went up his driveway to the back. True enough, the bird feeder,which was half-full when he looked out the kitchen window that morning, was all empty. Opening the little side door to the attached garage, he went inside to the shelf where he put the bird seed, grabbing a plastic cup to put some in. When he stepped back outside, he saw he already had a customer. The young squirrel that came over daily to eat the sunflower seeds was waiting in the driveway looking up at him.

"Just a minute," he told the animal as he filled up the feeder. A few moments later, he was back outside, this time coming out of the kitchen with a handful of walnuts. Dan bent down and held out a walnut half, which the squirrel— with some hesitation—grabbed with his teeth and scurried to a spot near the feeder. He nibbled away, occasionally glancing up at Dan as he had his afternoon snack. A minute

later, the squirrel ran to the lilac bush and Dan went over and dumped the rest of the nuts on the brick he put under the feeder with the sunflower seeds. With the pigeons lined up on the roof behind him, Dan decided to step inside again and let his guests dine in peace.

Walking to the front hall, Dan picked up the bundle of mail that he retrieved from the mailbox before his run. Despite his email activity, there was still plenty of snail mail advertising from the local grocery stores to the inevitable bills. He learned from experience never to pay them online. Then, there were the envelopes from various organizations asking for money.

As he sorted through the pile, he came across one from the Erie Policy Institute that had a really good grant writing position he tried applying for a few decades back. They didn't even call him for an interview. It was at the tail end of the time he wanted to, as they say, "make something of himself"—to no avail.

Opening it up, there was a letter from a Gayle Zimmerman in the most polite tone possible asking to support their upcoming fundraising drive.

His gift of fifty, one-hundred, or five-hundred dollars would make so much the difference. Don't these places ever get rid of a mailing address? With a smile, Dan crinkled it up, threw it in a wastepaper basket, and walked into the living room.

On the mantelpiece was a wedding photograph of his parents taken in 1948. The church they got married in was torn down later for I-77, the off-ramp located where the school was. Dan was born three years later. Right next to it

was another photo, in a brown frame, of Dan at age 15 with the family cat on his lap. It was taken in the living room of their two-bedroom bungalow on the West Side near the Reservoir; one of those Levittstown knock-offs built by the street full after the war. An only child, Dan had little family besides his parents and his maternal aunt, who would always invite him over.

Her family lived further out near the university, his uncle owning an engineering company. His five cousins rarely came over to Dan's house in return, since their fathers didn't get along. Besides, his mother was reluctant to have anyone over. Dan's parents always wanted to buy a brick ranch further out near Keaton Circle, but they never did manage to save enough money for a down payment. Other things cost so much in the meantime. Whatever education he got after high school he did on his own, with his folks helping here and there as much as they could. Working all day and studying all night, there wasn't much time for anything else. At least his folks were proud of him, for what it was worth. His dad told him so when he was in the ER that last time, so he was glad that he rushed over there when he could. It seemed that his parents thought about Dan more than he thought about himself.

At the other end of the mantelpiece was a large picture of Ralphie. Dan picked up the mixed-breed retriever at the county animal shelter 14 years ago when he was just one. Every weekend, the two of them would be fixtures on the trails in the valley. Dan would be in his baseball cap and lugging a backpack while Ralphie walked around looking for chipmunks or the occasional turtle to cross their path as cyclists sped past them. Most of his chatter at work was about his dog, and it broke his heart when he had to put him

down a little over a year ago. Dan never knew dogs could get cancer like people, and the thousands of dollars he put on his credit cards for the vet didn't lead to a cure.

Ralphie would have gone bonkers running around the yard of the new house if he was still alive. Dan could picture his pet running up to him every day with a ball in his mouth and then running to the back door so they could both play.

Walking into the dining room, he looked out the large bay window into the garden. The squirrel was back under the bird feeder methodically nibbling away at nuts and sunflower seeds, oblivious to the pigeons circling around him figuring out when he would leave so they could have their turn. Sparrows were flying above them, fighting each other for a spot on the feeder to get their share of the seed. Within half an hour, they would be all gone—the squirrel finally having had his fill, and the birds flying off at the sight of a red hawk. So, Dan finally had the backyard all to himself.

Except for mulching the beds and planting impatiens, Dan didn't do too much around the garden. If he had his way, he would cut down the tree in the corner of the lot to bring in more sunlight, plant some rhododendrons (blood-red) near the back fence, and start a real vegetable garden in the center. However, there wasn't any time. The previous owners left their grill near the gazebo and he did try it a few times this summer. If he knew people Dan might have had a cook-out, something he never did anyway. However, it was really nice sitting out there on the little patio drinking a glass of Southern Comfort at dusk watching the birds fly to the bird feeder and just relax for the first time in his entire life.

This time around, he just plopped down in the grass in the back and looked around at his property. There was a

blue jay flying from one of the trees as sparrows landed on the forsythia bush near the gazebo; taking turns flying to the bird feeder and quickly returning to the bush since he was out there.

The phone rang and he took it out of its case. It was his cousin Lucy, the one only of them who still bothered to call him.

"Happy Birthday Dan."

"Thank you, Lucy."

"Are you at the house?"

"Yeah, I'm just being lazy in the backyard."

"Did you get our card?"

"Uh-huh, and it's really nice."

"Glad you got it."

"Everybody doing okay?"

"Yes, as far as I know." Her three kids were all grown up and her husband was still talking about retiring.

"Have you heard from Terry?" That was Lucy's younger brother, now living in Oregon.

"I tried calling him last week and left a message."

"Oh."

"Jackie told me that she sent you one, too." Jackie was Lucy's sister, also younger.

"I got it yesterday. That was very nice," though she did write down, instead of Dan, "Danny"—which he always hated. It was the first time his cousin down in North Carolina did that in over ten years, and he stopped mailing her one as a result.

"We were thinking about having you for dinner, but you probably already have plans." That's what her husband Dave kept telling her anyway when she brought the idea up.

"It was a nice thought, though."

"Do you have plans for next Sunday?"

"You know me, I don't even know what my plans are for tomorrow," he lied. "But I'll call you later in the week, is that okay?"

"Sure. Anyway, happy birthday, Dan."

"Thank you. Goodbye."

"Goodbye?"

"Goodbye, see you later, and thanks again, Lucy."

He heard a small laugh on the other end. "Talk to you soon." With that, he hung up. Looking at his watch, Dan saw he had only a few more minutes before it was time. He got up, brushed the grass clippings from his pants, and walked inside. Opening the cabinet above the counter top, Dan took out one of the crystal flutes that he inherited from his parents. The small bottle of champagne he bought a week ago was chilling inside the refrigerator next to the chocolate cupcake he picked up at the bakery yesterday, so he went and took those out, too.

Heading into the living room, he sat himself on the

sofa, put everything on the coffee table, and glanced up at the clock. Putting one candle on top of the cupcake, he lit it and quickly blew it out without making a wish. Popping the cork off the bottle, he poured the bubbly into the glass, only barely preventing it from going over the rim. Raising the glass, he stared at the bubbles rising to the top in the bright amber liquid.

"Happy Birthday," he said out loud and, with a nod to the photographs on the mantelpiece, drank the bubbly down and then ate the cake. He finished the rest of the bottle a few moments later.

As he went to the stairs, he looked around at the rooms and all that he put into it that past year. Yes, the house was something he always wanted when he was younger. If things worked out like they should have, Dan would have lived here for years and sold it by now for a condo in a retirement community down South, or Avon. Well, things weren't meant to be that way.

Glancing at the grandfather clock, he saw what time it was. Steeling himself, he headed upstairs to the master bedroom. The sun's angle was such that the room was quite sunny. The room was so much bigger than the one in the other place with its one window overlooking the street. The previous owners did some major updating as well, putting in a walk-in closet and the adjacent master bath. However, it was he who decided to paint the room white; cotton sheets was what the salesman at the paint store said it was.

It has provided a nice background for all the furnishings in the room, from the chair in the corner from his old place to the new king-sized bed with down pillows he bought two months earlier.

Going over to the desk, he decided to put some papers in a drawer. The top was clean otherwise. As he opened the drawer, he saw the bundle of old photos that he was looking at the night before. Why did he put them in there? Taking them out, he glanced through them again—seventy years of life. Where did all the time go? There was a time, not too long ago, that he would wake up for work on a Monday and say he couldn't wait for Saturday. An entire year has felt like a week, as if he was ever speeding towards some finish line with or without a prize at the end of it. Flipping to the next photograph, he looked at a black and white photo of himself as a six-day-old baby, taken at the hospital where he was born.

The edges were a little frayed, and the writing in the back had faded, but Dan as a newborn, with a whole life ahead of him, was there for all to see. A sudden rush of sadness hit him in that sunny room, a brief second of despair that he quickly suppressed. What was the point of feeling sorry for yourself now? He knew what he had to do and that's that. He threw the photographs back in the drawer and closed it shut.

Taking the pistol out of the drawer, he sat on the edge of the bed looking at the clock. In five minutes it would be fifteen to eight, and he officially turned seventy. Dan propped up the pillows on top of each other and got comfortable on the bed. The sun will be setting soon, and fall was around the corner. He liked Fall almost as much as he did spring. A quick glance at his watch and realized it was almost time. So, he picked the pistol back up, and aimed it inside his opened mouth...

My Chocolate Lover

by Louise Francis

Intelligent,

Sensual, sweet and fine.

Got me feeling like a

Schoolgirl,

Falling for the first time.

The sound of your smooth voice

Makes my spirit

Soften and smile.

The organic, orgasmic

Chemistry shared,

It simply drives me wild.

My Chocolate Lover

Delightful,

Yummy in every way

Excitement fills my frame

At the thought

Or reference of your name.

When we a not together

Miles apart.

I crave for you much.

Yearning to see your face,

Taste your lips

Feel the melt in your touch.

My Chocolate Lover

Candy boy,

Jones for you night and day.

There's bliss in moments

Spent with you,

Addiction can't explain.

Nine Kings

by Kora Sadler

In a place not far away,

traveling I-77 North,

near Erie Lake,

Kings roam through the city

known as The Land,

when darkness falls upon them,

they appear like ghosts at midnight's hand.

So here's a story,

I'm going to tell,

pay close attention,

I hope it ends well...

There was a young woman,

a pretty one I may add,

she rebelled against her family,

she was very mad.

She left the Emperor's Palace,

to start a life of her own,

The Monarchs forbade her,

and the Princess lost her throne.

Trying to figure it out,

she stopped at a bar,

a stripper named Platinum,

approached her from afar.

She told her not to fret,

don't dim her diamond star,

Club Heaven was hiring,

she didn't need to look far.

With a smile on her face,

and a sigh of relief,

Princess took that hell job,

to get on her feet.

In the windowless club,

the night she could not see,

she danced to her own beat,

she knew they were eyeing her,

like wolves hunting meat.

As the beat slowed down,

she saw a glare in V.I.P.

she saw him poppin' bottles,

a handsome Prince,

with diamonds in his teeth.

He motioned his guards to step aside,

he saw her tight body, she looked like a dime.

Princess slid up and down the pole,

to catch the Prince's eye,

she stopped for a moment

so he can see her moves,

while she slowly slipped and slowly slide.

The presence of Kings,

were visible from far and wide,

the powers-at-be showed up from the north,

the south, the west, and the east sides.

The 9th King didn't show up,

he was drinking earlier, he's late;

the brake lines went out in his ride,

now there's eight. [8]

The 8th King was gamblin'

in the back of Club Heaven;

He got shot for shortenin' Platinum,

now there's seven. [7]

The 7th King was choppin' lines

from them Columbian white bricks;

He chopped himself a half,

and now there's six.[6]

The 6th King was shootin' dope

and getting high;

He got f*cked up on Seven's

Coke & Fentanyl

and now there's five. [5]

The 5th King was tryin'

to even 8th's score;

He pulled his nine on Platinum,

and now there's four. [4]

The 4th King became an informant

for the police.

He didn't care about the street code

"snitches get stitches"

and now there's three. [3]

The 3rd King hid from the police,

his secrets they knew.

Three can't keep a secret,

and now there are two. [2]

The 2nd King watch the rising sun;

with tears flowing from his eyes,

his body was flung,

from the rooftop of the building

where his chaos was done,

the village people cheered,

and now there's one.[1]

The last one is left all alone;

remember the Diamond Prince,

at the beginning of this poem?

Naturally, you would think,

he did it, he's the one!

The Prince takes over the land,

because the Kings are gone.

But he's not the heir,

not at the end of this poem.

As logical as that theory seems to be

he won't be the one

to take over the streets.

The blocks were deeded

and torn down one-by-one

because a Queen named Princess

is the new monarch of the throne. [Q]

One Week

by Steven Pryce

The ambulance took me from my parents' home in Canton to Cleveland. It felt strange, not having anything physically wrong with me. I sat up in the gurney, uncomfortable. I wished I could drive there. My dad, a hospital administrator, wanted to keep it a secret so I could still get a job. A lot of people at the hospital knew me from volunteering there. I was twenty-six years-old, and thought everything I wanted was gone. My last job was at a top national insurance company in Cleveland.

On the highway, I looked out the back window of the ambulance, believing everyone knew about me. I thought I was being exiled. My thoughts were racing. It seemed like cars were following me, and that the hospitalization was a way to institutionalize me. Maybe even get rid of me. Was I crazy? I was on my way to the hospital psych ward. My dad cried when I left. One EMT was with me.

"I'm uncomfortable," I said. "I'm not really sick enough to lay down for an hour."

"Is that all?" he said.

I nodded. "Yes."

"You're doing fine," he said.

At arrival, the two EMTs walked me to the elevator saying nothing. I didn't know what was going to happen next. I wore khaki pants and a button-down shirt with a barn jacket over it. My duffel bag was over my shoulder. I still thought I could die. I had never met a mental patient.

"Where's the patient?" the nurse asked as we got off the elevator and walked toward the nurse's station.

No one said anything, so I raised my arm. "It's me."

"I thought you were the case manager," she said.

"What's that?" I asked.

The nurse then asked me what medication I stopped taking and what I had. It was my first time there, I didn't know. I shrugged my shoulders.

"Hmmm," she said. "I think I can handle this."

We talked about the Crisis Center, and the questions they asked me there. I did believe that I was under surveillance by the FBI.

She asked if I was working, and I said no, but I was looking for work. "I think we can keep you on just one medication," she said. "I want to see if this works."

My empty wallet and keys were put in a locked safe deposit box. My duffel bag was checked too. "You can put on something more comfortable," the nurse told me. "If not, we can get you a hospital gown." She pointed down the hall. My room was the last door on the left side.

I walked down the hallway, noticing the pictures on the walls and carpeted floors. It was almost like a hotel. However, there were no televisions in the rooms. I visited people in the hospital before, and they always had a TV. I changed into my sweat clothes and laid down on the hospital bed, adjusting it up and down until I was comfortable. I put it at a forty-five degree angle to read, but it was strange. It felt straight, like I was sitting upright. My mind was occupied, so I couldn't read. A nurse then delivered my first dose of medication. "You won't feel this immediately," she said. "It takes time."

I thought it could be poison or hallucinogenic, but I wanted to trust the people who put me there. "Is this a mind-altering drug?" I asked. "Yes," the nurse replied flatly. "It is a mind-altering drug." I took it and she left.

My roommate then walked in. He was my height, with a thinner build and mustache. He looked to be in his thirties. "Hi," I said. "You must be my roommate." He said nothing and looked down. He approached my bed and made a sexual advance. I declined, and he laid on his own bed. I had no problems with the LGBT community, but he made me uncomfortable. I never met him before. Maybe I should put the rails of the bed up, or sleep on my stomach. I decided to report it. At the nurse's station, I explained what happened.

"What do you have?" the nurse asked.

I shrugged.

"What's your diagnosis?" she continued.

"I don't know," I said. "I'm not sure I have anything."

"What's your name?" she asked.

"Steven Pryce."

She then grabbed my file and read it.

"Okay," she said. "You can go back to your room."

"That's why I'm here," I said. "I don't want to go back to my room."

"Okay," she said. "Then I will have to do an investigation."

She called for another nurse and they walked down the hall toward my room. I followed them, thinking my roommate would just deny what happened.

"You can go back to your room," the nurse said again.

"I'm fine," I said.

The nurses stood in front of me and asked my roommate about what happened. He admitted to it. "Thank you!" I said, raising my arms in the air. The nurses gave me my own room. They put him in the room across from mine with another roommate. The next morning, I opened my door and his roommate threw a sock at me. He was put in the seclusion room with twenty-four hour surveillance.

I never saw my roommate again.

It was Monday morning. I missed breakfast, and wanted to know what was happening. So, I went to the nurse's station. The seclusion room monitor was to the right of the front desk. It looked like a portable black-and-white TV. "Don't look at that," the nurse told me. "Okay," I said. "Where can I take a shower?" She pointed down the hall. "It's the door on the right," she said. "You will see it."

I found it. It was a utility closet converted into a bathroom. The shower had a plastic base rather than a fiberglass shell. The shower head was on a hose. There was no mirror or sink; they were in the rooms. The toilet was a foot away from the shower. The shower curtain touched my back when I went to the bathroom. I grabbed my towel, underwear, and socks from my room. I would probably be wearing my sweat clothes all week.

After my shower, the nurses announced on the intercom that occupational therapy would begin at 10 a.m. I didn't have a watch, and there were no clocks on the floor. Again, I went to the nurse's station. "Are you going to be a problem?" she asked. "No," I said, quieting down. "I just want to follow the program." She said it would start soon at the end of the hall. "Alright," I said. "I will be there early."

At the group, we made art projects. I carved the face of an Indian into a copper sheet with a wood tool. The occupational therapist suggested I smooth out the lines, but the copper was becoming thin. I pressed too hard into it. Then, I was given a clear cup to fill with layers of colored sand. I tried to make a design. "It's best to keep it simple," the therapist suggested.

My thoughts were slowing down and I was becoming less fearful. "When are we going to talk about what we will do when we get out?" I asked. "Get out?" the therapist said. "Well . . . these are things you can do when you leave."

We had lunch afterward by the TV lounge. It was good. I've always liked hot food and a square meal.

On my tray, I found a menu card and golf pencil to place my dinner order. I checked off everything I wanted. No one else did. At the bottom, I requested chocolate cake for dessert and wrote, "Thanks!"

That afternoon, we had free-time. I used the exercise bike by the lounge area to stay in shape. It was noisy. A few patients left, but one female patient used it after me. I felt less different. "You're the first person to use that since I've been here," the nurse said as I passed her station. Dinner was announced on the intercom. I hoped I would get what I ordered. I sat down and was served. Everything was there. I began to eat, but worried that my food was tampered with.

"Are you gonna eat your chocolate cake?" a large, disheveled woman asked, sitting across the table. She wore lipstick. It gave me some calm.

"Yes," I said. "I don't get chocolate cake that often."

"You're supposed to say I can have your chocolate cake," she said.

I pulled it toward me. My parents then arrived. I was

surprised to see them after one day. They were dressed in nice casual clothes, nicer than what they usually wore.

"Who are the movie stars?" the woman across from me asked. I turned away.

"I have never heard that before," my mom said, smiling.

I took my tray to an empty table, and tried to explain to my parents that I didn't belong here. My dad asked what the nurses said. I told him about the medication, and that it took time.

"I'd do what they say," he replied. Later that evening, I took the medication again.

"How is it?" the nurse asked, much nicer now.

"Getting better," I said.

"Is it working?" she asked.

"Probably," I said. "I still don't understand why I'm here."

"You will," she replied.

Tuesday, I made it through the routine again. Instead of occupational therapy, we had group therapy. My ex-roommate's new roommate was now out of the seclusion room and in my group. He was neither showered nor shaven, but had some of the same paranoid thoughts that I had. His stories were like what happened to me, but I could see now that it was not normal.

"Would anyone like to comment on Brian's experience?" the therapist asked.

I kept quiet. He explained that he had been in the hospital before, and didn't understand why he had so many problems. "Do you take your medication?" the therapist asked. "Sometimes," he replied. "We can start there," the therapist said. It felt less like people were against me, but I wasn't ready to talk.

During meals, I continued to check off the menu cards and eat. During free time, I pedaled the exercise bike and walked up and down the hallway, wondering where the other patients were. The ward was locked, so I couldn't leave. Accidently, I bumped into a middle-aged woman opening her door.

"I'm sorry," she said. "Mind if I walk with you? I feel like I'm locked-up here."

"No," I said. "I mean I don't mind. But, it's not much of a walk."

"You had me worried for a minute there," she said.

She held my arm by the elbow. "I need stability," she said.

"That's okay," I replied.

I began to feel relaxed, and loose at the knees. I started to walk on crooked legs. She then gently pushed against me. "That's my husband," she said, as an older man approached. He was short, wearing a ball cap and flannel shirt. "You okay?" he asked, as he guided his wife his way. "Sure," I replied, and they left.

I became even more relaxed, losing some muscle control. I grabbed the arm rails on the walls to walk, but couldn't make it back to my room. So, I sat on the floor against the wall.

"Get up!" the nurse yelled at me.

"I can't," I said. "I feel funny."

"Get up!" she yelled again. "We're not supposed to touch patients."

"I need help," I said. "How about that orderly?" I asked, pointing to the man standing next to a gurney.

"No way!" he said. "I'm not touching him."

My dad arrived and came around the corner. Seeing me on the floor, he picked up his pace. "What's going on?" he said. He grabbed my wrist and took my pulse with his watch. "What kind of place is this?" he said, walking briskly to the nurse station.

"He's doing this on his own," the nurse said.

"Did you feel his pulse?" my dad asked.

"We can help him, but we need his permission." the nurse said.

My dad helped me up and walked me to the nurse station. "This wouldn't happen at my hospital."

"We'll take care of this right now," the nurse said. "Now, what can we do for you?" she asked me.

"I'm having a hard time moving," I said. "I think it is the pills you are giving me."

"How's your head," she said.

"It's okay," I said. "I didn't bump it."

She   smiled.

"That's good," she said. "Now what can we do for you?"

"I think I'm being drugged," I said. "I want the antidote."

"I have the antidote right here," she said. "Do we have your permission to use it?"

"Yes."

She took a syringe and injected it into my arm. My dad stabilized me.
"You should be okay now," she said.

I stood straight up and waited a minute to move.

"Will this happen again?" I asked.

"The medication is strong," she said. "It also affects the nervous system. But you should be okay. We'll keep an eye on you."

My Dad was too angry to stay around. He marched off to the elevator. I followed him, but the elevator doors closed automatically. So, I went back to my single room and slept. The next morning, I met with the psychiatrist. He wore nice, casual clothes, but with a tie. He spoke with an accent and had trimmed longer hair and a goatee.

"Do you know why you're here?" he asked.

"Yes," I said. "I'm beginning to understand it."

"Great!" he said. "You respond well to the medication. There is a chance you might do well."

"Thanks."

"So, tell me about yourself."

I told him about college and my last job. I thought I was being matter-of-fact, but he took it the wrong way.

"What makes you think you are so great?" he asked.

"I don't really think that," I said. "Maybe that's why I'm here. I did get an insurance job at a young age."

"Well I do this," he said.

"That's great," I said. "Can we talk more about what I'm doing here?"

"You're doing well," he said. "Better than most patients. What does your dad say?"

"He's not too happy," I said. "He also thinks you should tell me what I have."
"What do you think you have?" he asked.

"I have no idea," I replied. "It's probably bad if I'm here."

"You have schizophrenia," he said. He then asked me if I was suicidal or homicidal, which made me feel worse.

"No," I replied.

Shortly after, I finished my lunch and walked the hallway, hoping to talk to someone. There were empty rooms and closed doors. Slowly and casually, I walked to the nurse station. "You're doing better," the nurse said. "What can I do for you?"

"Where is everybody?" I asked. She pointed down the hall toward the elevators. "In there," she said. "It's the smokers lounge." I asked if I could go in. "I don't see why not," she replied.

The door had a wired glass window. Behind it was a grey, brown smoke that I couldn't see through. I opened the door, barely able to see the small, cafeteria-like room with rectangular tables and bench seats. I felt my way to an open space on the bench, accidentally touching a heavy-set man on the shoulder. I apologized.

"Can you see?" I said.

"I'll ignore that," he said. "You want a cigarette?"

"Not really," I said. "How long have you been here?"

"I don't have to answer that," he said. He flipped a single cigarette out of the pack. "Sure you don't want one?"

"I'm fine," I said. "I'm breathing in enough smoke already."

"Really," he said. "Take a deep breath." I took a deep breath and coughed.

"You can leave now," he said.

"Thanks," I said. "Maybe I will see you later."

Smoke billowed out the door as I left.

On Thursday, it was back to the routine. I took my shower in the utility closet. My clothes stuck to me as I left. I didn't want to walk down the hallway with just a towel. Group therapy was great. They gave us blue books for journals. We used them in college for essay exams. I wrote about the things that happened to me before my hospital stay. I showed it to the therapist.

"You should be better in a couple weeks," she said. "The medication takes a little time to work." I took back my journal, folding it in half and tucking it in my sweatpants.

On my way back to the room, the nurses were all at their station. "I guess we're getting a new patient," they announced. "He's being transferred from the prison. They think he will get better if he's here." I walked past them, looking away. "We wanted you to hear that," one of them mumbled. "I will be okay," I said.

He soon arrived. Two large officers walked him off the elevator, holding him under the armpits. He had a black nylon strap around his wrists, which they removed. I was curious to see him.

"Got something better to do?" an officer asked me.

"Yes," I said, pulling out my blue book. "I'm going to write."

"Good," he said.

The new patient had a scraggly mustache, with short hair combed straight down in front and cut close on the sides. He wore old blue jeans and a worn, red sweatshirt. After lunch, we had an exercise therapy session. We did squats, curls, and presses using wide, flat rubber bands as resistance. He closely followed everything the instructor said. It thought maybe he'd get better here.

"You like to work out?" I asked him afterward.

He shrugged his shoulders. "I guess," he said.

We were quiet for a minute, looking in different directions.

"I hear you're from...."

"Shhhh," he said, holding his index finger to his lips. I obliged.

"This place might be a little like where you came from," I whispered.

"Oh yeah," he said. "Ever been to prison before?"

We went our separate ways. At dinner, I was given a turkey leg, relish, and dressing. It looked and tasted like it was gourmet. "The kitchen staff wanted to make something nice for you," the server said. "Everyone else complains about hospital food." I ate slowly. Everyone watched me. My parents visited again, even though I was leaving soon.

That evening, I sat in the TV lounge and watched the news. Bored, I looked through the small library they had. It had books such as "The Trial" by Kafka and "Rise and Fall of the Third Reich." Slowly, I walked to the nurse station and asked about it.

"That's what the patients read," the nurse said. "Makes sense," I said, walking back to the couch. The news was still on, with world and political leaders. Before, I thought I would be one of them. I could get triggered.

"Hey," a tall black nurse with close-cut hair said. "Are you still up?"

"Yes," I said. "Just watching TV."

"That's good," he said. "You might do well."

"What?' I asked.

"All the other patients are in bed," he said. "Do you always stay up late?"

"Yes."

"Good," he said, handing me a paper cup with my pill in it and a Dixie cup of water.

"Thank you," I said, grabbing the pill and swallowing it.

"Is it really a—"

"Yes. It is a big deal," he said.

Friday was my last day. A nurse knocked on my door as I got out of bed. She cracked the door open and told me I would be getting a new roommate.

"That's fine," I said "I'm leaving."

"I just wanted to let you know," she said.

I took my shirt off and started to shave. The nurses

never removed my razors from my duffel bag, as they were supposed to. Some patients were at risk for cutting or suicide. My new roommate came earlier than expected.

"Oh great," he said. "I have problems with this." He took off his shirt too. He was a large man with a heavy torso. He looked like he had worked on a road crew. His mustache and hair were starting to grey, but he had large, tattooed arms. I wiped off my face and smiled. He became mad, and walked up the hallway. I was glad I was leaving.

"I guess you're okay," he said upon returning. He jumped in his bed.

"I'm out soon," I said. "The place is yours."

"I hope so," he said.

Outside the door, two nurses talked about me. They wondered if I was working or married before. "He was just working," one of them said. "Maybe he will get a job." I got depressed. They knocked on the half-open door. I had one last meeting with the residents and psychiatrist. Then, I would be discharged. I packed my bag and was ready to go. "Follow us," they said.

We walked to the other end of the hall. The three of them sat around a small table in a room like mine. The psychiatrist introduced everyone, and I was asked to take a seat.

"How are you doing?" the psychiatrist continued.

"I'm fine now."

He allowed the residents to lead the meeting.

"How was your stay?" they asked.

"It was fine."

"We are going to be doctors," the resident said. "You can tell us what is on your mind." He was thin and wore a white button-down shirt you could see through, and a black pattern tie with black pants. "Go ahead," he continued. "You can talk to us."

"Okay," I said, and talked about my roommate and other problems. They looked at each other and were quiet.

"People in glass houses shouldn't throw stones," the thin resident continued.

"But I'm a patient," I said.

"And what are you here for?" he said.

I told him what I had, and asked if I could leave.

"Are you having any more paranoid thoughts?"

"No," I said. "Can I go now?"

They looked at each other again.

"What did you do before you came here?" they asked.

"Sales," I said

"Your family is waiting for you," the psychiatrist said.

"Thank you."

My dad arrived with my mom and brother. My sister was a chef in New York City and couldn't make it. Embarrassed, I followed them into the elevator. There were no hugs or handshakes. "Awe Steve," my Mom said, patting my shoulder. We then drove to the Twisted Olive. "It's your favorite restaurant," my dad said. I was wearing my nice, casual clothes again. My blue book was folded and stuffed in the back pocket of my khakis. I wasn't better yet, but my dad wanted me to start looking for work. "You have been unemployed long enough."

The Origins of Titanium Squirrel

by Brett A. Tipton

It was a brisk spring morning in the woods. The birds were singing their lullabies. The deer were scampering over the mat of leaves covering the forest floor. And then, I saw him. All the squirrels know who I'm talking about when I say, "Him." Perched high in the top of the mightiest red oak in the forest, there he stood—Titanium Squirrel.

He was the mightiest of all the superheroes. He stood nearly thirteen inches tall. Sure, he may be smaller than all those other guys in capes, but thirteen inches is a towering height for a squirrel. Plus, he had the suit. It gloriously glimmered in the midday sun.

My name is Nugget. I've had my own adventures, but today I want to tell you about my hero. The stories of his escapades could fill volumes, but this story is simply about his humble beginnings.

It all began in the lab of Toni Sparks. I know. I know. Her name sounds a lot like that other guy with the red suit. But, that guy isn't real. He's just some guy from a comic. Who knows, maybe that's where Toni got the idea for Titanium Squirrel's suit.

Toni was the founder and CEO of Veterinarian Bionics and Robotics Lab. We call it VeBaR for short. She helps disabled animals by fitting them with prosthetic devices. She is a crack surgeon, robotics expert, and rumor has it, she is even helping to develop canine robotic technologies for dogs that help soldiers on the battlefield. With that background, let me tell you the story of the origin of Titanium Squirrel.

A crash reverberates through the lab. Toni spins around to see what caused the ruckus. She peers high above the lab floor and notices the opened window. Then, she sees poor Grey Tail lying helpless on the concrete floor.

She runs over. "Oh, poor fella. You must have fallen at least twenty feet. Well, at least you're in the right place." She bends down and puts her ear near Grey Tail. "You're still breathing. Let me take you over to our scanner and see what's wrong. Relax, little fella. I'll be as gentle as possible."

Toni gingerly picks up Grey Tail and carries him over to the scanner. "This will only take a minute, little fella. We'll get to see what's hurt."

Toni looks at the monitor and a tear begins running down her cheek. "I don't think you're going to make it, little fella. It's probably best I put you down as comfortably as possible."

Toni gently strokes his tiny body. Their eyes meet. "You want to live, little fella? I can see in your eyes you're a fighter. It will be a long and painful battle. You have a fractured spine, bruised kidneys, a punctured lung, and your tail is broken in three places." Grey Tail grimaces on hearing the news of his tail. He gently nods.

Oh no! Not the tail! This is Nugget. I know. I know. I probably shouldn't interject commentary. As narrator, I should be as transparent as possible. But, you have to know how serious a tail injury is to a squirrel. Most squirrels don't recover from a serious tail injury. Without the tail, we lack counterbalance. It throws our equilibrium out of whack. Plus, the ladies love the tail. Okay, maybe we shouldn't get into too many details about that, and just get back to our story.

"I can see you want to fight. Okay, fella. I'm going to put you under and perform surgery."

Everything goes black for Grey Tail.

Grey Tail opens his eyes. He peers around the cage and chirps.

"Oh, you're finally awake. You've been in a coma for six weeks. I guess now we find out if you're going to make it." Toni opens the cage.

Grey Tail stands. His legs quiver, almost collapsing under his weight.

"Take it easy, little fella."

Although wobbly, he gains his footing. He looks at Toni and shakily waves his tail.

"Oh, thank God. I feared you'd be paralyzed. The fact you can move is good. It means your nerves are still intact."

Grey Tail struggles to meander out of the cage and walks a few steps on the lab floor. His legs collapse under him.

"Oh, that's okay. You're doing great, fella. Take it easy. You need to gain strength a little at a time."

A tear wells up in my eyes. Yeah, yeah. I know. I should quit the commentary. But, this part of the movie is great. I know what you're thinking. "This isn't a movie."

Maybe not yet, but once Grey Tail's story gets out, there will be a movie. And here is where they'll introduce the hero's theme song and give us the training montage.

You'll get to see Grey Tail climbing things, and quickly darting about changing directions, and lifting heavy objects—like sticks and buckeyes. It will be glorious. And, when he's regained his strength, then we get the suit. Okay, okay. I'll quit the commentary and get back to the story.

Toni peers into Grey Tail's eyes. "You're doing so well, fella. You've grown so strong over the past few weeks. It's almost time to release you back into the wild. Maybe before you go, I should give you a gift."

She shuffles through the laboratory looking for a gift. Then, she sees it:

CHIHUAHUA SUPER SUIT

Toni chuckles. "Oh, that's crazy. I remember when that general wanted a super suit for a Chihuahua."

"It won't work," I said.

"Oh, it will be great. A Chihuahua will be a great asset on the battlefield."

Everything to that man was an asset.

"No, no, it won't," I said.

He looked me right in the eyes. "Do you know how stealthy a Chihuahua will be? We could sneak them just about anywhere. Just put them into one of those little dog carriers. A Chihuahua in a super suit. Our enemies will never know what hit them."

"It's not about size."

"But, Chihuahuas are so portable. It will be great!"

"It's not about portability."

I looked that dumb, dumb man right in the eyes.

"It will never work. Chihuahuas just don't have the temperament."

"Oh, sure it will work. They're dogs. Every dog is trainable."

More trainable than many men.

I looked him in the eyes. "It's not going to work, but if you insist, I'll build the suit."

I mean, why not. Do you know how much military contracts pay? Sure, he should have listened to me. I'm only the world's foremost expert in veterinary sciences. But, what do I know?

"Poor Pepe. That was the name of the suit's first and up to this point only owner. First time he took flight—BAM! Crashed headfirst into the Bell drive thru. Then, he peed himself. But, this suit has just been discarded and sitting on this shelf. Do you want to try it, fella?"

Grey Tail shakes his tail. Every squirrel dreams of flying and being super strong. How could he not?

Toni opens the box. The glorious suit glimmers in the sun shining through the window. I pee myself a little. Sorry. I know. I know. You don't need the extra commentary, but this is so exciting. This is the unveiling of THE SUIT!"

"Okay, come here, little fella." Grey Tail jumps into

Toni's arms. "This suit is covered with pure Titanium. Underneath the Titanium is a Kevlar liner. These little things on the back are thruster packs. They'll let you fly. Plus, the suit will give you super strength. It's all powered by quadlithium. I know it sounds like Star Trek's dilithium, but quadlithium is a real thing. The military has been developing it for years. This power pack will last a hundred years."

Toni carefully fits the suit to Grey Tail. He skillfully flies a loop around the laboratory. He lands gingerly in Toni's lap.

Their eyes meet for the final time. Grey Tail points his tail towards the window high above the laboratory floor.

A tear flows down Toni's cheek. "I know, fella. It's time for you to leave."

Grey Tail wraps his tail around Toni's cheek and gives her a gentle caress. Then he flies out the window—no longer Grey Tail, but now the greatest superhero ever:

TITANIUM SQUIRREL.

Pandemic Sits at the Table

by Jodie West

I. Spring 2020

The anxiety sits with you
at the table, lying indolently near
the platter of vegetables, fried
in its own grease of unease.
It is there next to you on the sofa,
curling the dish towel in your hand
as you speak with your elderly parent,
your jocular tone belying the fear
you have for him, fear he has
no problem extracting from his
eighty-year-old mouth, in the lingering
list of activities in which he no longer
allows himself to indulge.

Four deaths in two weeks, he says,
everybody dying, and his fear an odor
that transmits itself through the towers
of our cellular phone connection,
emanating from his body, his mind,
to mine, manifesting itself in the discussion
he has about troubling with his house
after he is gone.

II. Summer 2020

We cannot but help the coming back,
to the same point on the same arc, he and I,
tracing fingers over our fears
and back again, like the hummingbirds
that use the same nest, adding more
materials on top of the older ones.

Unease demands a return to contemplation
of it, older materials forming a base
for the nesting spot of this fear,
yet unlike the birds, the uneasiness circles
and returns despite the discomfort
of its nesting.
And rifling amongst all of this,
pressing at one's back like stones
tied with leather, is what will be there
when things realign themselves
into some semblance.

A pandemic that will become divided
into the historical befores and afters
of significant human events.
To meet again, as whatever form emerging.

III. Autumn 2020

And as the months crease into
unending lines, one stacking aimlessly
on top of another, some build fortresses
to wall selves in, whether they be made
of brick, mortar, or wood, or the inability
to access the deeper parts of the static

in which they find themselves.

Many lay traps in the mundane
and make excitement out of saccharine
and overburdened sharing with relative
strangers. Such exposure
dismantles the beauty of secrets
and imagination's prize.

How then to discover others
under the banality of the online?
That is a savor all its own, but one
whose risk can formulate the scents
of the seasons and the miracle
of remaining in touch while yet
unable to brush another's hand
with the wisp of one's own.

IV. Winter 2021

Construction on four lots within
a half-mile radius of home adds
its own unearthly scents to things.
Noises of industry may be pleasing
As strident signals for the future,
possibilities for additions
to the dwindling masses of visible
humanity amidst the unceasing
sign of a pandemic,
notches of distraction to add
to the wooden limbs of life under
a self-imposed lockdown.

V. Spring 2021

And then-
In tandem with spring blooms
we—much of the mass of us—
venture out, permission granted
by the changing of color tiers,
moles poking noses from underground,
squinting at the wonder of the sun,
markings of freedom

surprise at the joy
of brightness, some charging
like runners at the start of an April
marathon, flinging boldly
through restaurant doors
and cinema entrances, grasping
those distanced as we find
the lifelines we thought lost
dangling between interlaced fingers.

Others—like me—content to bask
in the newness of extended stays
granted, refreshing sun-deprived skin,
then returning to dwell in the comfort
of the microcosm our homes have become.

Peepers

by Diane L. Johnson

I couldn't believe I talked until two in the morning, jaw-jacking with Theresa about her old flame that was desperately trying to make a comeback. Sheish! Some people just can't grasp the meaning of the phrase "it's over." Anyway, eager to know all the details, Theresa and I chatted into the wee hours like it was a Saturday night. Needless to say, this morning, I slept a half-hour past the second time I hit the snooze button. But thanks to Peepers, my wise old kitty, I woke out of a peaceful sleep. She did what my alarm couldn't do; gently pouncing on my shoulder and meowing in my ear.

"I know... I know." I mumble, kissing Peepers. "I shouldn't have stayed up." Peepers just pounced from the bed to the floor, disappearing to who knows where. Rushing to dress, I was surprised I had time to wash down a piece of dry toast with the last of the 2-liter of Coke. After checking the alarm, making sure all the bells and whistles were on, I reached for my briefcase on the breakfast bar.

"Come on Peepers! I don't have time to play with you this morning. I've got to get going." I said, nudging Peepers to move her rump off my briefcase. She just yawned and gave me a look, as if to say, "You talkin' to me?"

"Peepers! Please!" I groaned. "You know I can't be late another day, or you and I will be taking up residence at the local shelter. Now, move your behind!" I demanded, tugging at the briefcase. Raising her head, my kitty, my best friend in the whole wide world, rattled every bone in my body, when she retorted. "I don't think so!" Now standing on all fours, and I flat on my behind—as I had tripped over the bar stool from the shock of hearing my kitty speak—Peepers didn't seem to be bothered in the least that I was paralyzed and couldn't move. I guess that was a good thing, because she was just getting started as she continued to speak.

"Listen up, Honey," she sneered at me, digging her paw into my briefcase—the only thing I owned that was real leather. "If you go to work today, you're going to miss the opportunity to share in the 350-million-dollar Mega Jackpot via the blessings of Russell." Peepers hissed. "Unbeknown to Russell, one of the tickets that he purchased last night is the winning ticket, and he is going to give that one to you. He should be coming through the door...hmmm, in the next thirty minutes."

Grabbing the plastic grocery bag that was so conveniently lying nearby on the floor, I began breathing slowly into it as I listened to Peepers. She was on a roll, and I was trying to take it all in before I passed out. "I don't know about you," she said, staring me down, "but I'm tired of living in this dump and eating off-brand kitty food."

Meowing, Peepers continued to voice her feelings. "I'd like to be toted around once-in-a-while in one of those travel bags Paris Hilton carries her mutt in. And, I'd like to have a cat pole and comfy bed of my own." Letting out a soft purr, Peepers hopped off the briefcase and paced back and forth on the breakfast bar. "So," she said, "if you leave before Russell gets here, your old-dude is going to change his mind and keep the winning ticket for himself. Annnnd your sweet

Russell is going to dump you and take off with the chick downstairs in Apt B."

"But..." I began. Purring, she stared me down with those steely gray eyes.

"If you stay, we can dump this place and kiss Russell's lazy behind goodbye and get on with living our new lives."

Now, jumping to my feet, I shouted at the top of my lungs, "Are you saying Russell is cheating on me?!" A startled Peepers hopped from the counter to the computer desk. Arching her back, she hissed, "Look, don't go clamming up on me now!" I gave Peepers an icy stare, and she purred for a couple of seconds more before leaping into my arms.

Her warmth tempered my outrage. A sudden peace came over me. Tucking Peepers close to my body, we headed to the living room and took a seat on the tattered futon. Not voicing another word, it was as though we both could read each other's thoughts. Softly stroking Peeper's silky fur, I asked her if she wanted to watch the animal channel. She whimpered a meow. Snuggled together, Peepers enchanted with her favorite show, we waited patiently for my 'old-dude', Russell.

Planet of the WHAT!?

... A Quite Horribly Fractured Fable

by Mindy Altrid

Preface

Solitude

Joseph paced until he could no more. He cooked one more meal and ate...ate in solitude of any other human being. Joseph was a prisoner, or so he seemed to be. He had witnessed over the span of only a few days the death of the human race. He was now a prisoner of loneliness, fear, and desperation as he ultimately knew he would be next, the last human to inhabit the earth.

Preface to the Preface

Does Earth Exist?

What do you think? If all mankind were wiped from planet earth, or any other planet, or the moon, or other planets' moons, would anything really exist? You know, like if a tree falls in the forest and there is no one around, does it make a sound?

If you are like me and like to ask these fun and silly philosophical questions and want to spin around in circles with the angels that inhabit the head of a pin, go ahead and try to answer them. But perhaps you prefer the more probable reality, that of unhuman, not inhuman(e), life

continuing in mankind's absence. Of course, I said more probable reality, not certain reality, but let's move forward on the "probable" premise.

***

Okay, whether you are Darwinian or favor "Intelligent Design"-inian theories of where and how life emerged, if all other species, plant, animal, microbial, amoebial, slimemodial, and whatever continued to exist, how would it? Would another sentient, hopefully one of better overall nature than current man, come to the fore? Now, I know we could get into a long debate as to whether man is intrinsically prone to good or prone to not give a damn about anyone but his/her personal self, but remember—he/she/they have been wiped from the face of the earth and any other planetary body that we know of, so that is a moot point!

A more intriguing question, at least to me, is what remaining species will dominate, not necessarily in a bad way, or will human beings re-emerge in the course of time, which leads us to...the re-emerging story of the battle between Godzilla and Gigan! No, no, no! That's not right. It leads us to the story of...

Planet of the WHAT!?

... a quite horribly fractured fable

by Mindy Altrid

Chapter One and All

Suzy and Her Baby

Now, Suzy is an orangutan, and not just any orangutan. Hold it! Cut! Oh jeez, how schmaltzy is that? Suzy was a friggin' ordinary orangutan who just happened upon the open door of an abandoned fertility clinic...of course it was abandoned, all the humans are dead...as she was foraging for some oranges. She had happened to smell the sweet scent of the luscious fruit, her favorite, emanating from somewhere inside the building. Following the fragrance, she was led to a small room filled with metal canisters labeled with numbers.

Suzy couldn't find the oranges but was intent on doing so. The fragrance filled the room. She hadn't noticed the atomizer filled with the pungent scent on the solitary desk standing in a corner, but as she followed her nose, she found the source. What a disappointment for her. Finding no oranges, she kiss-squeaked madly and repeatedly while flailing her arms in all directions. Now, although Suzy was pretty ordinary for an orangutan, she was no dummy. She had been born in the circus and had been trained to

recognize numbers from one to ten. Not for the hell of it, to be sure. The circus was out to make a buck or two or three, like anyone else. The numbers training was for the act she was in, which was to do the amount of backflips based on the number shown to her.

Of course, she received a reward for doing the correct number of backflips. Bet you can't guess what. Na-nana-boo-boo! Oh, you're all smarter than I thought—yeah, oranges! There just so happened to be ten canisters in the room all labeled from one to ten with big bold numbers that any idiot or ordinary primate could recognize. Unless this sounds a little too coincidental, I assure you it's not. Before you could put a nickel in the Nickelodeon, she was doing backflips until she was silly. This trained performance tired her. Finding a chair next to the desk, she sat. Having now performed those fifty-five friggin' backflips (feel free to check my math, you overachievers), she was bound and determined to find the real oranges that had to be hidden in the room. Besides, she was hungry as hell.

***

Meanwhile, back at the ranch…No, we're not goin' back there! The phrase doesn't even make sense with no humans around, and I told you they were all kaput, in other words, dead as a doornail. Okay, so you argue that there must be a "somebody" around somewhere—maybe in some deep cave or one of those doomsday shelters built to prevent annihilation by the god-darned government.[1]

Argument over! One last time. They're all—every last one of them—dead! In fact, the carrion poachers of the world, the real Hell's Angels of earth and sky, the Angels of death without a sickle, put an end to every last decaying morsel in two shakes of a turkey vulture's tail.

***

Suzy...you do remember her, don't you? If you don't, you maybe stayed at the ranch a little bit too long even though I told you not to. Perhaps the deer and the antelope lured you in to play God knows what with them...Well, Suzy was still at rest. Her heart and respiratory rate were gradually returning to normal. She took a big sigh to expand those few last reluctant lung sacs, otherwise known as alveoli if you want to walk around all proud of yourself with an expanded head to match Suzy's now filled air sacs. Her head now cleared from the excess carbon dioxide, which had slowed down the electrical communication between her brain's synaptic clefts, allowed her eyes to spy more numbers. She was about to get up and do a repeat performance, but she resisted for two reasons.

One, she had not found or been given any oranges for the last performance, and although she was ordinary, she wasn't stupid. The other reason was pictures of little children. The same kind that used to love watching her perform her circus act, all bubbly with smiles and bright

---

1*My apologies, or rather my thanks, to Roger Miller for the score of Big River.

eyes, maybe with a little drool, but that was cute, too. You might think this odd, but seeing the pictures of the children on the bulletin board along with the numbers, not all the numbers, mind you, filled her with a melancholy. She missed performing in front of the children, but it was more than

that, but she didn't know what. What could be making her feel like she wanted to hump like a banshee in heat? No, she wasn't stupid, I already told you that, but she was horny. Why the emotion and the lust? Well, let me "splain it to you, Lucy." We'll let Suzy figure it out for herself. Suze...We're going to get informal now, since we all know Suzy pretty well by this time, and besides we're going to get very personal... Suze had turned age twelve in the past year but wasn't privy to the workings of pubescent female orangutans, being she was raised in captivity, and her mother passed when she was only three. She never knew where mommy went but was always suspicious of a specific male handler with a lascivious look on his face.

Truth is, the handler hit upon her mother repeatedly over the span of several weeks, giving her an infection that killed her. But let's back away from that sordid story, wash our hands, spray water on our eyes—maybe our whole brains, and get back to Suze. She had missed the maternal caressing and she certainly had missed the maternal breast! Yeah, the human hands that now fed her were fine, but a fake nipple on a plastic bottle didn't hold a shine to warm native teet. Suze had needed to be bottle-fed by human hands for four more years. Most of those hands had been human female hands and none of the women looked like her own mother. So, there went being able to identify with a female of her own species. That left her hormonally clueless, save for the bitchy behavior her female handlers exhibited from time to time (she would learn being bitchy was acceptable because there was "a reason.") She hadn't realized flailing her arms like when she didn't find any oranges was her form of "bitchy." I know a few women who do that, too. Wonder if it's a primate family lineage thing.

"We've wandered away from the initial cause of Suzy's melancholy," you say. Au contraire, mon ami! Read on.

Oh, and let's not forget Suzy's horniness. Yes, she was craving intercourse without knowing why. She did know every time she looked at the pictures of those children next to the numbers she could not resist feeling a maternal desire, and a simultaneous netherworld dampness...actually, it was more like someone forgot to turn off the faucet.

She now associated her maternal desire to the pictures of children and her horniness. Now, I know I told you earlier this primate was ordinary, and then I added, not stupid. Well, I lied. She was a bit quicker than your average bear, or orangutan actually, for that matter. She studied the bulletin board with the numbers trying to figure out why only some of the ten numbers had pictures of children while the others didn't. She wondered if it was a clue to finding the oranges. "Why back to those darn oranges," you say? Come on, you have to remember primal urges—food always before sex. Hmm, I guess you can actually take that two ways! She was quite famished now with her sexual hormones raging as they were. She looked at the pictures again as if looking for clues. She noticed that with each child was a tank, a canister, just like the ones resting right near her and each labeled with one of the numbers. Now, she didn't know how to associate numbers, children, oranges, and lest we not forget, the current leak in her undercarriage...for the life of me, I wouldn't know either...but in her famished state any and every strange brain synaptic connection could and did happen at that very moment.

Not being able to make full sense of the thoughts that flooded her threw her into a frenzy. The next thing you knew, she was banging tank number one with the wrench that was

attached to its side, trying to get it opened. Failing, she violently threw the tank against the concrete wall, only to have it bounce off while making a loud clang and then landing at her feet. She began to flail her arms again in frustration while thinking, *there's got to be oranges in those tanks!* She put one of her orangutanian index fingers to her wide simian lower lip and began to think. *How do I get into those tanks?* She tried banging with the wrench again until her ears rang. Frustrated, she was going to launch the wrench across the room when it dawned on her she had seen this tool before. In fact, she'd seen it many times when the circus tents were put up and taken down. The humans—the now defunct humans—used them. They would attach them to something. She didn't know what, but when they cranked them, the tents would stay up or come down.

Well, this little bit quicker than average ape didn't take long in figuring this puzzle out. Looking at the round cylindrical tank, the only place she saw that could be a match for the wrench tool was the top hexagonal fitting. She attempted to place the wrench and after several tries, voilà! The tank stood open, spilling out a cold white vapor over its top edge. At first, cautious of the rolling vapor, she bent down and put her nose to it. Quickly she pulled away, as like Jack Frost, the cold nipped at her nose. She bent down again and put her sniffer close, but not as close as before. She said, "Baba baba beh beh, baba beh beh," which, translated from the common orangutan dialect, meant, "Damn, it don't smell like oranges." In fact, it didn't smell like anything at all. She turned the tank over in a huff and a vial dumped out, clicking and cracking on the floor as it bounced.

Seeing the Cracker Jack prize, she picked it up but immediately dropped it as a biting cold stung her fingers.

She whipped her head around and stared at the picture of the child with tank number 1 as she attempted in a monkey business way to make some sense out of this mental cacophony, but the only thing that happened was a feeling of motherliness to go along with a resurgence of her wet, sloppy horniness.

Suze became agitated again, having no clue what she was desiring and yearning for, but she knew now it wasn't for oranges. Hormonally in rage, the great ape was now berserk, instinctively looking for whatever it was that could satisfy her —sort of like a food craving where you go to the fridge, open the door, and stare until the lightbulb almost loses power, except, unlike you at the fridge door, her heart was racing, her nips were firm and tingly, and she was wet. Yes, I said it again—she was wet, wet with desire for something she knew not what. Does that "what" whet your sexual appetite? She was now a red-haired locomotive, the loco being most operative here, on steroids—female orangutan sex steroids to be more precise. With arms waving contortedly, she was now a raving banshee in heat, jettisoned to that state by simply seeing a picture of a child with a cylindrical container. Ah, you're saying to yourself, *It's the shape of the tank that's causing this reaction in her!* I suppose you could be onto something, Sherlock, except she's never seen "one" before!

Besides, this tank is about 100 times bigger than a male orangutan's mem...Hmmm, perhaps you're right after all in your summation, counselor. Well, anyway, this raving banshee of an ape was tearing down and apart everything that wasn't screwed...yes, I chose the word screwed, as it was appropriate for the subject matter...down. She looked as if she was withdrawing from heroin, wildly looking for her last remaining stash with a blindfold on. Chairs went flying;

tables, research equipment, and bookshelves tumbled, and finally, Suzy was about to tear all the pages from the manuals when one of her wild eyes...no relation to Hall and Oates' private eyes...spotted a pornographic picture of two humans engaged in you know what.

She instinctively knew what this was. It was what she was craving. She quickly became addicted to looking at all the pictures. It probably would have been better if Suze knew how to read, but since "every picture tells a story, don't it," and since "a picture's worth a thousand words," she really didn't have to. You're probably thinking, *What the hell is a research and fertility lab doing with pictures like this?* Tell you the truth, someone with a sense of humor thought it would be funny to add this to the rest of the technical info in the manual, and many a new person to the lab was seen wide-eyed and then disappointed to not find more of the same in the following pages.

But there were other pictures, and that is what Suzy was looking at. From this series of pictures she learned of egg development, egg retrieval, sperm and fertilization of egg by sperm, early embryonic cell cleavage...take your eyes off her chest; there ain't no breasts in this picture...and then the whole cryogenic process. The second manual detailed the process of introducing an embryo or multiple embryos... excuse me, but that makes me want to sing, em b r-y-o, em b r-y-o, em b r-y-o and embryo was its name-o...into a uterus for pregnancy. Noticing the same type of vial in the manual as she had dumped from the canister made her pause. Once more, she put her finger to her lip. Uh-oh, you say? Yes, little Miss-more-than-ordinary had certainly put two and two together. She poked at the vial she had dumped onto the floor. No longer cold, she picked it up, but noticed it had

leaked out all of the fluid inside. *Not to worry,* or *bahehe hakuna matata,* she said to herself in orangutanese, *There should be four more tanks, numbered 2 through 5...*from primates, in this case human primates...*that already had succeeded in having babies.*

No dumb bunny was she. She knew to trust the pictures, the numbers, and the tanks that produced, and not the ones that showed no sign, no kiddie pictures of success. Heck, she was smarter than most humans I know! And rather than just grabbing the tank numbered 2, as most of you probably would, Suzy reviewed the pictures of the kids again and picked the tank that corresponded to the child that appealed to her the most. Remember that beauty is in the eye of the beholder, and all beauty isn't skin deep. Okay, enough of the proselytizing. Suze actually chose like you might if you went to an animal shelter for a pet. Reminds me, I believe, of a Twilight Zone episode where aliens abduct a few humans and put them on display in one of their zoos—no creature comforts at all, mind you. If this is weirding you out, relax. Remember, you're dead—all trace of humankind are gone— well, except for pictures and memories, and Suze had both. She chose based on the warm feelings she got from the pictures, and those warm feelings came from the kind things that she had experienced with her human trainers and with the other animals she had met while in the circus.

Almost wants to make you cry, doesn't it? For those of you who already are, grab your hankie and dry your eyes, because this story must go on. Suzy picked tank number 3. This was not the booby prize, and Monty Hall's or Wayne Brady's audience would have been ecstatic and envious with the ensuing outcome. The only thing better would have been had Suze worn a silly costume while choosing. Now that she

had chosen the tank, and knowing that she had inadvertently destroyed the embryos from tank 1, she wanted to make certain she didn't destroy the embryos from her precious, her now coveted "precious" number 3. As the moment was hot, and she was, too...remember, she was in heat...she knew she must strive to satisfy her overwhelming desire for motherhood. She quickly went back to the manuals and reread how to safely defrost the frozen embryos. But how was she to introduce them? The pictures only showed humans using special instruments to do so.

She started waving her arms around and turning in circles. She added a few backflips, too, but it got her nowhere. Breathing hard, she sat quietly and thought. Yeah, the index finger was back on her lip. She had it! *All I need to do is find something small enough to carry those embryos to leave them deep inside of me,* she thought. *Maybe the field mouse that followed the circus from city to city,* she wondered. *I bet he's small enough!* She ran back to the circus tent...yes, the tent was still standing...let me remind you, only the humans were obliterated...found Maury the mouse, and convinced him to give it a try. Maury, having had mousy sex before with his little pecker and loving every second of it, was more than willing to try a total body immersion experience. Suze, not sure how he was to carry the load into her, left it up to him. Also, not knowing for sure if he would be successful, as the manuals said all transfers did not always succeed, she decided to have him only transfer two embryos from a total of four in the tank.

Not wanting to crush the embryos with his paws, nor wanting them to accidentally become dislodged from his fur if he were to embed them on his back, he decided to carry them in his mouth. Once inside, he found it to be very dark.

Although not being able to see, he just marched forward in her wondrous self-lubricated tunnel of ecstasy. Being so jacked-up, he couldn't help but spluge once before he got to his destination. But when he reached the back wall door, entry was denied.

No effort by him to bore his way in with his pointy nose was accepted. Even being covered by a combination of vaginal efflux and his own seminal juices would not allow him to squeeze through the tighter and narrower channel which led to his destination. Frustrated, defeated, deflated, and above all, disengorged, he backed his way back through the tunnel that had been his delight a few moments earlier. Clearing the secretions from his eyes, he then stared at Suzy forlornly and said, "Sorry Suze, I couldn't squeeze into your womb. I tried every which-way and every position, even the fetal position, but no-go." He tried to spit up the embryos he had stashed in his cheeks, but they seemed to have dissolved in his saliva. Oh well—two more potential fully developed humans gone. Gone with the rest of them. Will they ever inhabit and dominate the earth once again, the narrator asks rhetorically, urging the reader to continue further into the dramatic tale.

Groaning with utter disappointment at the failure of her tiny friend, Suzy wondered what other friend she could ask to help. There were certainly other animals, like the lions, the tigers, the bears, oh my, and even horses and elephants, but those were way too big. Maybe what she really needed was to get Goldilocks to find her an animal that was just right. No, no, no...that wouldn't be appropriate to inject a fairytale character into this realistically true story. Finger to her lip again, eyes to the heavens, and she had it—

Ludwig...that would be pronounced, Lude-vig[2]...the trained flea! Again, she ran back to the circus tent to find her tiniest of friends.

"Ludwig, Ludwig," Suzy bellowed, hot, in more ways than one, and out of breath. "You've got to help me!" Ludwig barely stirred, as he had been taking a long nap. In utter boredom he had fallen asleep, the flea circus act had been in limbo since his trainer had suddenly vanished. Ludwig was clueless of the demise of the human race, as there was still flesh of other species to bite. You could say he couldn't see the humans for the flesh.

"Ludwig!" Suzy shouted...sorry, that should be she shouted, be-bla. Please correct Suzy's previous bellow on your own. Ludwig groggily shook off the cobwebs from his eyes—not real cobwebs, mind you. Real ones would have been a nightmare to a flea. Seeing Suzy through half opened eyes, he snapped, "What? Can't you see I was sleeping?" Just so you know, fleas speak perfect English. With arms waving like a lunatic, Suze, sans apology, squeaked, "sque-squeak, squeak, squeak-squeak, squeak."

"You wish me to do what!?" replied Ludwig, his eyes fully wide now.

Suzy repeated her series of squeaks, which when translated said, "I want you to travel up my vagina and put two human embryos in my baby bucket."

Suze actually shied away from using the word vagina, saying "hoo-haw" instead. It made no difference to Ludwig. He knew exactly what she meant, and excitedly stated he was all in—literally! He also, literally, jumped at the chance,

_____

2* Okay, so I'm no phonetic specialist, but my phonetics are apropos to the story.

quickly landing in her nether region.

For him to be invited to a warm and wet veritable flea paradise would be like Heaven, Nirvana, Shangri-La, and Valhalla all rolled into one!

With saliva leaking from the corners of Ludwig's mouth, Suze laid down the ground rules. Using an English translator this time, she laid out the whole plan and added important pieces from the story of Maurice's failed attempt. Ludwig listened attentively while still salivating throughout, although the flow gradually ebbed when he was told biting would be off-limits. Explanation over, he didn't realize just how impossible his mission would be, but he understood it, chose to go engage it, and then destroyed the tape that had never been recorded. He had one question and one statement when Suze was done. The question was, "If Maury wasn't able to get in, what makes you think I will?" And the statement, which he said emphatically, was, "If Maurice's saliva destroyed the last two embryos, we have to find a different way to get them to their destination."

If you may have noticed, none of these characters from this circus are imbeciles. In fact, they're downright friggin' geniuses! Yes, with flaws...maybe not in your opinion...but geniuses nonetheless. Ludwig had an idea. "Excuse me a moment," he said, and hopped back to his abode, where Suze had found him dozing earlier. A few seconds later, he returned, carrying his fleabag. Yeah, I said "his fleabag." What of it? He packed his cargo tidily away and proceeded to take one more hop, this time like a heat seeking missile, to his dewy channel of blissful intrigue. Don't get all hot and sweaty now. Remember, this was his job, his mission. This was work. And you don't need to tell me that whoring is work and an occupation. I know, but ol' Ludy wasn't getting paid a dime!

Ludy bided his time getting to his destination. Heck, why wouldn't he? We know you all would, unless you're afflicted with the "premature" thing. Oh, you know what I'm talking about. Don't make off like you don't. While he slowly luxuriated in splendor, he began to feel subtle vibrations. They repeated over and over in the same cadence. *Were they the gentle contractions of Suzy's vaginal musculature helping propel him to where he needed to be as if he were a sperm helped in its swim upstream,* he wondered? Strange, but he didn't seem to feel any movement forward, although the vibration became stronger and stronger. He finally realized the vibrations were coming from Suzy's increasingly loud voice as he could now hear her words. For the sake of time, let me leave out the bleh-blehs. She was repeating over and over and louder and louder, "Are you there yet? Are you there yet?"

Ludy was going to say, "Be quiet, kid, or you can get out of the car and walk," but realized she was the car. He tried to answer her, but she couldn't hear him, and she finally gave up. Ludy quickened his pace, sensing she was communicating a need for haste. "Ho he hum, ho hum, ho he hum..." he sang as he trodded, or was it skipped, forward. Remind me to ask him when he returns from his journey to the center of where life begins. Okay, stop it! Let's not argue. I know many of you believe life begins when the sperm meets the egg, and that's already happened here, so let's move on, little doggies. "Ruff" you say? Yeah, life is rough. What about it? Come on, let's go find a different scene, and scenery, for that matter.

Ludy found it easy to squeeze through the tiny uterine escape valve. He unloaded the cargo from the flea bag and placed it high into Suzy's womb—high to lessen Suze's chance of hemorrhaging when she birthed. "Asshole, I'm never going to forgive you for this pain!"

"Don't blame me! You asked for it!"...her precious babies. It was time for Ludy to make his descent, but when he got to the pubes protecting the castle, he dangled in the forest branches and considered moving his residence and paying Suze rent to stay in her sultry humidor. He dropped the thought when he realized he might be squished to death when she eventually delivered.

***

Tank number 3 turned out to hold a wonderful baby and Suzy eventually gave birth without a whimper. Nine months had been a long time, and Suzy was surprised when her baby—not babies, one didn't make it—arrived with little to no hair anywhere. She had forgotten he was human. Not to worry, though. She was planning on raising him like an orangutan as it was in her nature to do so, including breast feeding for eight years. Surprised!? Scandalized!? Must I remind you, again? There are no human beings to criticize and pass judgement on this innocent child and his mother. As to the name, as you probably know, or should I say, as far as anyone knows, humans are the only species to identify with names. "Oh, not so fast, Kowalski!" you say. "Some birds have names given to them by their parents," you say? Okay, I don't trust that as far as I can throw it, but I'll use it. Let's get back to the name, and if birds can do it, I'm figuring orangutans can, too.

She decided that repetitive "blehs" were a bit too boring for her beautiful baby. Besides, it was kind of, you know, bleh, so she livened a short but sweet bleh with a melodious squeak to produce a wondrous-sounding name. It truly became music to anyone's, anyone in the animal kingdom besides the now-extinct humans other than you know who, that is, and if you believe plants can hear, then them also. Now, if you must know, if you must have me translate it for you, here we go...ready? Deep breath. Letting it fly and attempting to capture imperfectly the primal animal essence captured in Suzy's native utterance, I sang, "Niiiiiiiiiiiiiinesti-ei-ei-ei-ei-ei-ei-ine."

"Ninestine? That's not melodious at all," you say! Not the way you said it, it ain't. I had given it my best shot, but it's like what happens when you translate a beautiful-sounding song from its original language into English.

***

Now, as we say, life must go on. It really doesn't, but this story must go on. Quickly to its end, you implore —"please, oh please...please!" Uh, uh-uh, my little word imbibers, I will torture you slowly to the very end...uh, uh-uh!

Ninestine grew strong and eventually did grow hair. The hair became a wild mess on his head. I know what you're thinking...I think. Well, maybe not yet, but I will attempt to make you think it. He was smart...got it, yet? No!? Okay, he was exceptionally bright...??...Oh my lord...Alright, Ninestine was a friggin' genius!

But what sort of progeny would you expect from an extraordinary ape? Oh, you argue she supplied none of the genetic material, you unbeliever of nurture over nature. It's true—Suzy hadn't supplied her own egg in the development of little Ninestine, but that was a distant and fading memory now. It was a fading mammary...no, not mammary—heh heh —memory. She was not done with her breast feeding. She had at least six more years to go. Anyway, it was a fading memory until young Ninestine posted on social media his mother's fertility story. "What!? That's way too far-fetched. This is not only slow, but unrelenting torture," you say? Well, let me also 'splain this to you, Lucy. I must admit, you were right. Most of Ninestine's smarts had come from his genetic parents.

You ever wonder why it is that children have become so facile with computers since the Millennial Generation came to be? Exposure maybe was part, but it was not the main reason. It was part of evolution! There was a widespread genetic mutation possibly due to some cosmic event like a pulsar...I don't have a clue what a pulsar is, just go with me here...that affected most of the population at that time. I say most of the population because some had been spared the pulsar effects as they had been testing out their secure, radiation-safe underground bunkers in case of alien or government attack. Why do you think the book "Computers for Dummies" was written? Bless all their control-alt-delete souls. It's for all those that had been shielded from the radiation—God truly may have helped them if they were still alive.

Okay, where were we? I think we we're at Ninestine's post before we got sidetracked, but I must say, it was a necessary detour. Unfortunately for you, but I guarantee you'll appreciate it, we'll have to take one more sidestep before we go racing down the track. Up 'til now, you might be thinking that Suzy was the only orangutan in the world. She may have been in isolation at the circus, thinking she was the only one in the world, but you know that wasn't true; unless you are one of those who believes they are the only living entity in the universe and everything else exists purely from their imagination. You know primates aren't stupid, so, when left in the world without human dominance, wherein they were restricted to either tropical forests, zoos, and the circus, they expanded their territory; and, in the process, stumbled upon electronic devices, including cell phones and computers.

Like most of us, whether mutatedly irradiated or irradiatedly mutated or not, who still hate to read manuals, rather relying on trial and error, they did the same. One of those primates was an aging and childless great ape from a small zoo not more than walking distance from where Suze and Ninestine had taken up residence. Quick aside here—remember Ninestine was still exclusively breastfeeding, but for Suzy's delight she had found an estate on which to live that was teeming with fruit trees, especially her favorite orange trees. There were other trees, too, as well as proteinaceous insects, which provided her a healthy and balanced nutritious diet and no need for supplements. Learning of Suzy's success of having an in vitro pregnancy, this aging but infertile ape was blooming with hope to ripen with child. Lest you think this infertile orangutan didn't have a name, I assure you she did. Not to get wrapped up in native pronunciation again and all that blah blah blah, or rather bleh bleh bleh, let's just call her Betty. Oh, by the way, if you want, you can call Ninestine "Al."

***

Betty soon arrived at Suzy's fruitful estate. Suzy was expecting her since she had received a bleh-mail from her the day before. Betty was anxious to get started right away but was disappointed to find she needed to be in heat for it all to work. No problem. All she had to do was wait, right? Right—that is, unless she was never to be in heat again! Betty would be thirty in six months, prime age for complete senescence of any fertile capability.[3] Being the nice jolly orangutan that Suzy was, she offered for Betty to stay with her and Al until it was time to transfer the now frozen bundle of joy. This delay gave them time to plan, unlike with Suze and her fretful frenzy in her time of heat. Suzy showed Betty the pictures in the manuals that spoke tens of thousands of words that even an ordinary orangutan like Betty could understand. Don't get me wrong—although Betty was average, she was also sweet, and Suze was happy to have another female orangutan around. The delay also gave Betty time to choose which tank she wanted her embryos from. She fell in love with a picture of a baby girl infant with pink bows stuck to her head. No hair, just all skin and bows! It would be tank number 4 for her.

***

Three months later, and still no heat. Betty was cranky and worried. Suze was concerned, but not as much as Betty. Betty was becoming increasingly dry (you know where). Suze was wet with milk, for she was still lactating. Betty was...enough of this already! They consulted the manuals once again, and found they could rev Betty up again with fertility drugs and hormonal supplementation. They would exaggeratedly manipulate and extravagantly

---

3* If you didn't understand that, refer to the book, Fertility for Dummies

synchrodate her cycle. They would energize her, tenderize her genderizer, enhancerize her fecunderizer. A couple weeks of this, and they were ready for "I-day,"—implant day. For us, a couple more seconds of these spoonerisms would have led us all to vomit from hormonal overstimulation. Ludwig the flea had been salivating for days after getting the new request for his services. He played it cool, even asked for compensation since he was now a pro. All he wanted was a few bites while traveling down the love canal, but Suzy would have none of that. She knew from the manuals that any risk of infection could spell doom for success. Ludy accepted anyway. He accepted his warm dewy journey would have to be compensation enough, but no amount of hollering and vibration was going to rush him this time. He had brought his ear plugs.

Now, after opening tank number 4, the merry band of novice endocrinologists and near novice impregnators were resigned to make a critical decision. You see, tank number 4 had only one embryo remaining. Should that embryo not make it, poor ol' Betty would have to go through another round of painful injections to rev her up again, and she didn't wish that.

Betty studied the pictures from tanks 2 and 5. She chose 5. She would have preferred sticking with number 4, but knew she would be taking a risk. It's not like she didn't like the picture of the child with tank 5, but she didn't get as many of the warm and fuzzies as with 4. Luckily, there were three embryos available in tank 5. Although risking a greater chance for twins, even possibly triplets, Suzy, now the grand experienced fertility guru, advised Betty to have Ludwig implant all three in the hope of getting at least one to take. Implantation again successful, Ludy leisurely made his way back to daylight. His tardy return trip invited yells and screams from the now two immensely incensed and sensitive apes who thought he had taken liberties—and maybe even some nibbles—which was expressly forbidden by their agreement. They had no idea that Ludy armed himself, or would that be "eared" himself, with a sound defense. How's that for a non-risqué double entendre?

They were all over him like flies on shit [4]when he emerged from his reverie. "What the f____ were you doing in there so long?"

He knew not to argue with a couple of hot-headed women, but he thought to himself, "What the hell did you think would happen when you invite a guy to indulge his whole friggin' body for the purpose of honey pot penetration?" He then asked if there was a place to take a shower and strutted off.

***

Betty had a touch-and go-pregnancy. Not only did she have to take the dreaded three-hour test to check for diabetes, which luckily turned out negative, but she developed toxemia and went into early labor. Good for her she was near her due date, for besides her baby being rather

------

4*Ludy deeply resented my use of this phrase since he felt I was disparaging members of the insect class. I needed to point out that their distant relation in no way reflected on himself, and in fact, and this was news to him, they were from distinct orders. He was from the royal order of Siphonaptera, and the fly from the lowly order of Diptera, only Ludy's order being related to Cleopatera, the ancient Egyptian black widow spider femme fatale. He felt so much better, smiled a piercing-sucking grin at me and bit my hand.

puny...not all skin and bows like the previously mentioned picture...she was otherwise healthy, exhibiting that health in a piercing cry, a cry like a fudgin' friggin' infantile wraith in training!

***

Life was fine for many years on planet earth for Suzy and her son Al, and Betty and her daughter, whom she formally named Jezebeth. The name had somehow mysteriously been implanted in her brain at about the same time little Bethie embryo was clawing its way into mother earth.[5] The name grew on her, just like her little pipsqueak, and by the time she was born, she liked the name; she liked how it sounded, [6] not in English, but orangutan. I thought you would have understood this by now!

Life was fine because the gestapo had been laid to rest —mankind had supped its last drink of its own polluted air. Somehow, everything seemed brighter, more colorful. Somehow? I just told you the air had become increasingly dingy and foul. Are you skimming through this story and not actually paying attention? Oh, you say you are paying attention and you're very concerned. Concerned about what? Hmmm, you're more astute than I thought. Yeah, I know these crazy lady orangutans have reintroduced humans into their midst, but they're so infatuated with their kiddos that

---

5* Best I make this clear for those not able to understand terms in context – Earth here is not dirt, it is Betty's uterine lining.

6* Levon didn't like the name. If he had a daughter, he probably

they see them only as they see themselves. "Oh shit," you say. "They're just as self-absorbed as humans were with themselves. This does not bode well."

Are you a complete pessimistic doomsayer who dismisses any likelihood of good in these two ladies and their ability to raise well-balanced, happy, and healthy orangutanian-human, or would that be human-orangutanian, children? Oh, you concede the children may be controllable when they're young but worry about what will happen when they become aware. Aware was pronounced slowly and with full hand and arm motions starting with clasped hands at the lower abdomen, rising up to the chest and exploding in an upward and outward unclasped reach to the heavens. Yoga freaks, I know you're in ecstasy right now. You then had better tell these experimental experiential mothers to throw themselves and their children into the dark ages, as in dark before any light from computer screens and cell phones, because becoming aware became precocious decades ago.

***

Did Suzy and Betty heed the warnings? Indeed, they did. They went totally gridless, trashing all the electronics. Not just the phones, hard drives, laptops, etc. With plenty of sustainable food sources on their estate, Suzy had welcomed Betty and Jezebeth to stay with her and Al.

They had no need to make contact with any other creature with more than half a brain (Less brains would be even better, so as to spare them from any attempt at special domination).[7]

Ah, for the return of simplicity, to the run-of-the-mill, survival-of-the-fittest, predatory relationship. The world would return to the simple food chain and not the crazy, messed-up, always-in-revision food pyramid that humans had introduced..."How many carbohydrates do I get to have with each meal? You know I love my carbs!"

Now, really, there would be no intraspecies murder, except maybe due to mental derangement from syphilis, but that would be more like manslaughter or murder by insanity, and not true murder. Intentional transmission of rabies, I suppose, could be grounds for the charge of murder. Although, I think you'd have to acquit an unintentional killing by a violent bite to the carotid while competing for a love interest.

Back to the Suzy estate...gridless life was heavenly, as heavenly as gridless life was for most women after the nineteenth century. Everything ran, you might say, smoothly —save for some bulges near the midsection, swimmingly... they did have a pool...like a well-oiled machine without any electronic or mechanical parts. Al and Jezebeth grew and became great friends. Then puberty hit. Although Al was two years Bethie's senior, she was the one who matured first. She busted out all over. Yes, indeed—busts, acne, hips, and, if you looked closely at the now long hair on her head that her mom let Bethie wear to her waist, you could see two little mounds

---

7* Special domination does not refer to special as in gifted, but rather to domination by any one particular species. Now, I guess that would be special, too, but it also could end up being preachy or dictatorial.

protruding, like two tiny head buds...and attitude, whoo, that grew to unfathomed conceited proportions. She was becoming a mean young Jezebeth!

Watch out now, she could chew you up, literally...and spit you out if she hated your taste! She even began reading tarot cards, without any training! She always peed in the swimming pool, stole Al's newly purchased cheap cologne, and constantly blamed him for her self-inflicted injuries, enraging him to no end. Al became so agitated, he began to have nightmares of what Bethie might do to him.

Suzy had no other choice but to kick Jezebeth out the door, for she was taking her toll on the peace and tranquility of their humble estate. Betty didn't want to leave, and she wasn't being told she must leave, but she didn't want to abandon her precious, her Bethie. She was convinced Bethie would outgrow this phase. She was sure it all was being caused by a bubbling cauldron of raging hormones. Boy, did Betty have that right, except she didn't know that the cauldron's vitriolic syrup would continue to course through Bethie's veins forever. This was no learned behavior. Make no mistake about it. This was all genetics. She would not outgrow it. It could not be removed.

So, out the door they went, in their birthday suits, not a fig leaf to their name, banished from the gates of Suzy and Al's existence and into the countryside for Jezebeth to wreak her havoc on the rest of animal and plantdom.[8]

Suzy and Al did happen to venture out one time from their paradise. They did so with trepidation, but they did so nonetheless. Suzy was both confused and intrigued as to how

---

8* If you'd like, I suppose you could call it omnidom.

her son, Ninestine, was of such good nature, while Betty's child was so quite the opposite...I'm trying to be nice here... Betty's child was a witch—plain and simple—but what in the hell made her that way? They made a short trip back to the infertility laboratory in ninja garb during a starless and moonless night to search the manuals one more time. Suzy looked at the pictures on the bulletin board, but two were missing—numbers 3 and 5. The other photos still hung in place, still showing the smiling children that had been born from the embryos used from the tanks. She remembered why she had chosen tank number 3 and how she had been rewarded with Ninestine—just what she was expecting and hoping for. She stared long and hard at photo number 4 and remembered there was only one embryo in the corresponding tank causing Betty to choose another. Perhaps Betty should have went with her first choice, her gut instinct, disregarding the risk involved with only implanting one embryo, but you know of "should 'ave, would 'ave, could 'ave." There ain't no do-overs. You get what you got. Sometimes you don't get what you want and not even what you need. But life goes on and you make the best of it, right?

Suzy looked down on the floor as she wondered how Betty and her offspring were doing, and there, in the corner, covered in dust, were two pictures with curled-up edges. They were face down with writing on their backs. Without reading what was written...remember, she didn't know how to read...she turned them over to see they were the missing photos—the photo that warmed Suzy's heart and the photo that had been Betty's reluctant second choice. Handing them both to Ninestine...he had learned the rudiments of English from a book he found on their property...he read what they had written on their backs.

On number 3 was written—child: Angela Lanzano

egg donor: Maria Lanzano

sperm donor: Lorenzo Lanzano,

On number 5 was written—child: Lia Mero

egg donor: Rosemary Mero

sperm donor: unknown, but with the odd characteristic of literally being horny.

The rest of the story isn't pretty, and I therefore will not tell it, for the tranquility found by Suzy and Al soon after the destruction of man was gradually lost as the screw was turned tighter and tighter and as the years turned a mean young Jezebeth into an even meaner ol' one.

THE END

Conclusion and Moral

Maybe it's better that we will never know if life truly exists outside the brains of a human, but if life and the earth would still exist it would very likely be better off without a lot of monkeying around.

Afterword

I first must say that the characters, especially Betty and Al... I say that because I have friends named Betty and Al... do not reflect on people nor orangutans in real life. As with many of the phrases I used throughout the story, they were inspired; and, in fact, taken from song lyrics, television shows, movies, or well-known phrases in common use. I do hope many of you recognized them.

Lastly, I must thank my friend, Dave. I think he's still a friend. This short story would not have been written without him. His response to my initial funky philosophical question which first appeared on Facebook drew his angst and the suggestion that I read my Bible. This is the truth, the whole truth, and nothing but the truth—as opposed to the story. Suze was torn between a name that appealed to her and was simple to say in orangutanian, and one which she just simply liked. You know, like Levon did. Translated to English, they were respectively Adam and Jesus.

Remembering Life After Death

by Alison McBain

I breathe in the new leaf smell,
warmed by the singing sun.
My feet are burning,
light and heat concentrated
through the filter of black sneakers,
butt parked on the front steps
of the empty porch,
facing the street's flashing-by cars--
a suburban afternoon
nearly touching April.

Last year, today,
the air was burning
in my shriveled lungs,
corroded by a newfound
viral child,
an unwanted pregnancy
that was killing me,
killing millions--

an enemy so small
it became too large to fight.

Sweat-soaked and chilled
I closed my eyes,
breathed through the fear
of my daughters, orphaned
by the end of my struggle.

Behind my lashes
the future showed teenage first-kiss
agony, tasselled caps
tossed into the mother-lacking air,
unhugged grandchildren--
thousands of hours, untouched
by my closed eyes.

The pause went on too long--
I had to remind myself
when to breathe again.
I smelled the burden of patience,
the acrid tang of perseverance
carried into the afternoon
and night
and day again.

My daughters asked questions
and I answered,
coughing words of love,
telling them the lies they needed--
that I was fine
that I would get better
that I would not die,
bitterness smothered under stories
I didn't believe
as I reminded myself to breathe.

I am still breathing
but it catches in my heart sometimes,
the better words I knew before
lost behind last year's fog.
The sunshine feels good, though.
It is Sunday
and my daughters are laughing
instead of crying.

The surprise of the season
is that clichés about spring
died this cloudless afternoon
and my sarcasm doesn't mourn them.
I am new with the greening daffodils,

the catcalling of birds,
relentlessly twerking bees.
Labor pains are put aside
with the abundance of birth.
I can park my butt on the porch,
sit in the momentary sun
and just breathe.

Shutter

by Russell Henley

I'm not a failure. I am accomplished. At fifty-eight years old I am already retired, living in a beautiful large home, married to a wonderful wife whom I very much love and who very much loves me, and I have a best friend named Watson who follows me around as soulful dogs do. I've been an achiever since childhood and now comfortably rest among the fruits of my labor. My concerns aren't many. I pursue a few hobbies that take up my days nicely as I want them to. I cook different cuisines. I garden. I putter around with my old VW van, which I've kept on the road since my college days. And, I indulge myself in a lifelong passion—photography. I'm not fantastic at it but I have won a few awards and sold a fair many prints. The anonymity of being behind a camera suits me well as I am an introvert by nature and choice.

My wife loves to travel. I do not. This difference between us takes a great deal of understanding on both of our parts. She has, though, a travel companion in her older sister, who lives out of state. Together, they travel the country, staying in Air BnBs and visiting everything from quaint historic towns to busy cities—from ice-capped mountains to sparkling gulf coast beaches. They tackled the jungle terrain of Costa Rica, just the two of them; out of cell phone service with only backpacks on their shoulders. They loved it. I can't fathom any desire to take such a trip. My idea of a trip is one that lasts a couple of days at a secluded cabin within driving distance of home.

I started seeing a psychologist about twelve years ago after a death in my family left me more than distraught. My grief lasted more than it should and only grew stronger with time. It interfered with my work and dangerously affected my marriage. I isolated myself more than usual. My world was crashing down around me. The only thing I could buoy was my success. As I said, I'm not a failure. To keep me that way, I took the sincere advice of my doctor and forced myself to get out of the house, pursue new interests, and challenge my mind. I even studied mindfulness and began to temporarily meditate. I stopped the spiral into the abyss and started to climb back into my old self. I dare say I'm even a better man for my journey.

The hardest advice for me to follow was to get around more people and to socialize to the point of developing actual friendships outside of the artificial ones provided by the work environment. So, when I heard about a photography club, I became interested. A club like that would meet the criteria set forth by my doc and still provide me a certain level of controlled interaction, while letting me enjoy my favorite hobby. So, after careful consideration, and when the time suited my mood, I went to my first group shoot.

We were to meet in the parking lot of the west overlook at a state park in the late afternoon, one hour before sunset. There, at the right time, and if the atmosphere favored us, we would be able to photograph a blazing sunset over the deep dark valley below our perch on the high bluff in the east. Only three other cars were there when I pulled in the gravel parking lot.

The cameras outnumbered the photographers. I had my camera strapped by itself around my neck, the strap wrapped around my hand as an extra precaution against dropping another one. Two people carried two cameras. The older man carried four. It became immediately obvious that he was the group leader. The others respected his ego. There was something oddly and distantly familiar about him.

We stood just a few feet from the sheer drop from the stone outcrop to the valley below. I walked over and took a peek down to see ancient boulders piled high where they had landed countless years before, after releasing their failing hold on the high bluff. I stepped back to the safety of flat terra firma and into the uncomfortable presence of the obnoxiously extroverted leader. As he talked, his familiarity grew. I tried, but couldn't place how I knew him. And then, it struck me. This blowhard was my eighth-grade science teacher!

Here was the man who introduced me to photography, the appreciation of science as truth, and the wonders of nature with all of its glory which surrounds us. There was a time in my distant youth when I practically worshiped him. I also unrealistically loathed him. He had given me my first lesson in failure. His lesson would follow me the rest of my life, and the anger I associated with it would rear its ugly head virtually every time I made a mistake. I am not a failure.

He liked to play games as he taught his classes of young, developing children. One day—my fateful day—he came to the end of his lecture. And, as an example of our immaturity in listening, he proffered a quiz. It was pass or fail. Only one student would take it. He challenged me. I accepted. The question: "What is the closest astronomical body to the solar system?" I replied that the small Megellanic cloud was the closest body to the solar system. I was wrong. The large Megellanic cloud is closer by about 40,000 light years. I failed the quiz and received an "F". It was, and still is, the only "F" I've ever received. I do not fail.

Exhibit A: a remarkably clear red-hued photograph taken just before the body fatally struck the boulders below the cliff, the image showing my palms still facing forward from the shove.

The Spider Tree

Carol P. Vaccariello, D. Min.

Aunt Rosemary, mom's youngest sibling, was terrified of spiders. We lived at 3567 East 147th Street across from Rickoff Grade School. I remember being asked repeatedly to recite that address in the event that I would ever be lost. Our house was a two-family. Mom and Dad and I lived upstairs. Gram, Gramp, and Aunt Roe lived downstairs. I was very young. Aunt Roe used to babysit for me. I knew she was terrified of spiders. Spiders didn't bother me. I could pick up daddy long-leggers. I marveled at their very long legs and wondered how they could walk without their legs getting tangled.

When my husband Frank and I lived in California, I witnessed a uniquely different spider experience. In the small room I used for my office on the second floor of our townhouse in Orinda, I was watching curiously as a spider seemed to take up residence on the ceiling above and behind my head. He wasn't bothering anything—or was it a "she?" I don't know the habits of spiders, so I let him live there, and literally hang out with me.

Days, weeks, months passed. I watched that delicate and persistent creature spin and weave, weave and spin— maybe a "she." I wasn't paying close attention to what she was doing, until one day, I climbed up closer to see what was hanging from the ceiling. There were several long, slender, cocoon shapes hanging there. I thought it was strange. She had them in a straight row. She had captured her prey and preserved them in cocoons for safe keeping.

Getting back to Arachnophobia; a deep fear of spiders. Here is a true story.

After my ordination to ministry, my first pastoral call was to an Interim position serving a church in Barberton, Ohio. At first, the folks weren't so sure about calling a *woman* to fill their pulpit. It didn't take long for our friendship to develop and the trust to grow. However, I had been called to be an Interim, which means I was there to help them prepare for their next full-time settled pastor. We did so well together that I couldn't convince them to establish a pastoral search committee to begin looking for their next pastor.

In frustration, remembering this was my first church, and I wanted to do everything right, I contacted the regional office to share my dilemma and ask what to do about their reluctance to begin a search. The determination was made that they would do a search, and I would be permitted to submit my papers to be evaluated along with other candidates. They called me and I served them for more years than any of their previous pastors.

During Seminary training, I was attracted to Clown Ministry. I attended workshop training, before realizing my dream to attend and earn my degree **Summa Cum Clown** from *Ringling Brothers and Barnum and Bailey Circus Clown College* in La Crosse, Wisconsin. The Barberton

Church became a training camp for Clown Ministry. Adults and children came for the weekend training. Each year, our Clown Troupe would march and perform in the parade. A highlight was the *Model T Ford* that some of us rode in or stood on the running board while puttering along. We had clowns of every shape, size, and age—even a clown being pushed in a wheelchair. Every year, we walked away with an award for being one of the best in the parade.

I was known as Posie the Clown. I wore a white face with a large smile. My hair was not blond—it was bright yellow and poker-straight; a tiny straw hat with a posie standing about ten inches straight up, hence my name. My costume was created with a large hoop at my hips, larger than a hula hoop, made of light spring steel that bounced freely when I walked or maybe waddled.

One sunny afternoon, I was working at the church and received a call. It was from a woman I never met who called looking for Posie the Clown. Occasionally, I would perform for home parties—mostly children's birthdays. Most often, I would offer Clown Ministry in other churches for banquets or special events. I thought this call was for a clown gig. Then, I heard the emotion in her voice. The conversation went something like this:

Me: "Yes, Posie, speaking."

Caller: " You don't know me. My son knows you. He is friends with one of the boys that comes to your church. My son is having a problem. Someone said that you might be able to help."

When I heard that a child was hurting, I listened with different ears. This mother explained through tears, "I don't know what to do. We have taken him to Cleveland Clinic, to the Counseling Center here in Barberton. He cries and refuses to go back." As I listened, I wasn't sure why this mom was calling me. Lots of children don't like to talk to counselors. What was so desperately wrong that spoke through her tears?

Then, she came to the crux of the problem: "My son has horrible nightmares. Every night, he screams over and over again. I go to him. I calm him. But the entire family is being affected. We can't sleep because of his constant screams. I'm calling you because someone told me that you know a lot about dreams and that you help people understand their dreams. Do you think you could help my son? Could you help us?" she added. "I think he might be willing to talk to you because he knows you are Posie the Clown."

Wow! No one had ever asked me to tackle such an important and meaningful task. I said, "I can't promise anything, and yes—I have worked with children's dreams. I would be glad to talk with him."

We arranged that he would come with his young friend from the church to meet with me. There would be no adults involved, only the two boys and Posie the Clown. The next day, I watched for them. Each of them a young nine years old. They were holding hands and swinging their arms as they walked up the walk to the front entrance. I met them at the door and invited them inside. They were so cute. He didn't know me without my clown makeup on.

His young friend introduced us. After a short visit, I asked if he would like to talk to me for a little while. When he consented, I asked his friend if he would like to go outside and wait so that we could talk. I offered to call him when we were finished. I was relieved to learn that the parents had prepared them for this, and the young friend was headed home instead of waiting alone for an hour or more. When he left, I noted that Christopher was considerably smaller than his friend. He appeared a little frail.

There was a tall winged-back chair in the office. I asked him if he would like to sit in the big chair. He smiled. He turned to face the chair, and, holding on to the arms, lifted one knee up to the seat and pulled himself up. While tugging up and rolling over to sit down, I heard a grunt, and it sounded like he was in pain. He scooted his hips back, his knees straight and his feet pointing directly toward me. His slight stature was truly emphasized as he positioned himself in that large embracing chair. I asked him how he was doing. He told me he went to the doctor and had a tube removed from his side and it was sore. I didn't want to pry, but I couldn't help but wonder about the tube he had removed recently. I tucked this tidbit away to pull it out when needed.

I moved right to the reason for his visit. I said, "Christopher, your mom told me that you have had some really bad dreams that wake you up and won't let you sleep."

He nodded, speaking quietly. "Yeah, scary."

I continued, "Mom, said you don't like to go to the

counselor. She thought I might be able to help you. Would you like to tell me about your dreams? I might be able to help."

He agreed with a soft "yeah."

I told him that Posie had a very special way of talking about bad, scary dreams. I explained, "When you are with me, I don't want you to be afraid, so we have lots of helpers to keep you safe from anything scary. What do you think about that?"

He smiled and I could see that he was wondering. I knew he had seen me do clown magic and he knew that I could do magical things. He knew I could make things disappear and reappear. I would venture he had a little more faith in my abilities than the counselors!

I started the Dream Work process with him that I have found incredibly effective, not only with children, but also with adults who suffer from night terrors or nightmares. In this method of working with dreams, I "see" the dream he shares *as if it were my own dream*. I don't see the exact images he sees. However, I stay in sync with what he is seeing and feeling. I am continuously checking with him to be sure we are still moving together along the same track.

I explained the plan. "Here's what we are going to do. I would like you to tell me your dream just like you are seeing it right now, the same as what you see in the nighttime. But here is the difference: I don't want you to be afraid. So, every time you begin to feel afraid, I want you to stop telling your dream and let me know that you are feeling afraid. Okay, will you do that for me?" He agreed with a nod.

"Christopher, close your eyes, just like you are sleeping. You have a movie screen in your head. If I say red, can you see the color red on your movie screen?" He nodded.

"Good. Now, start the movie of your dream on that movie screen and tell me what you see. Remember, if you start to feel afraid, tell me and we will get helpers to keep you safe. Okay?"

He closed his eyes. " I'm in the back of a truck, the kind that has the wood on the side. I can see out between the wood." I ask, "How are you feeling right now? Do you feel safe?" Christopher replies, "Yes."

I say, "Good, then tell the driver that he can start the truck slowly."

Christopher instructed the driver to start the truck and go slowly. I said, "Christopher, look around you. What do you see?"

"The road," he answered.

"Thank you," I said calmly and softly.

"Christopher. Do you see anything else?" I asked. "Look all around the truck. Describe everything you see. Are there flowers? Is there grass? Is it just dusty and no plants or buildings?" In his small voice, he said, "Just the road. No houses, no buildings. There's some trees. Mostly just dirt."

"Is it sunny or is it raining?" I asked.

His simple reply was, "It's sunny."

"Can you feel the sun? Does it make you warm?" He nods.

I watched his closed eyes. I studied his face, and every slight movement of his small, frail body. I wondered why he looked so unhealthy. The truck kept moving slowly. He went along for a while and then I noticed he began to get agitated.

He started to fidget. His small white hands seemed to tremble just a bit. Softly, I asked, "Christopher, is there something wrong?"

He answered quickly, in a whisper. "Yes"

"Do you feel afraid?"

"Yes."

I sped up my voice, lifting the pitch and volume. Speaking with strength, I instructed, "Ask the driver to stop the truck. Right now! And he will stop."

He called out, "Stop the truck!"

I asked, "Christopher, did the truck stop?"

"Yes," he answered softly, eyes remaining tightly shut. His head bent forward. I saw some of his tension soften. Gently, I asked, "Christopher, what made you afraid?" He answered, "We are getting closer to the Spider Tree." I didn't know what he meant. I could see his small body tense when he mentioned the Spider Tree. I waited.

"Christopher, can you tell me about the Spider Tree? What does it look like?"

"It's a big tree and there are big spiders crawling all over it," he explained.

"Christopher, who or what do you need to be with you so that you won't be afraid of the Spider Tree?"

He was silent. I knew he didn't understand what I was asking.

I asked in another way. "Do you want your Mom or Dad, Aunts, Uncles, Grandmas, Grandpas? Who can help you to get closer to the Spider Tree without being afraid?"

Now he got it. "I want all of them to come."

"Okay," I said.

One at a time, we asked his Mom, Dad, Aunts, Uncles, Grandmas, Grandpas, until his fear subsided, and he felt safe. I asked, "Are you ready to ask the driver to start the truck again?"

"Yes," he said.

I said, "Call out to him in a loud voice so that he can hear you. Ask him to start and to move slowly." He settled in with all of his family surrounding him and called out in a voice louder than I heard so far.

The driver started up the engine and the truck slowly began to move. Family members were in the back of the truck with him; his mother sat in the passenger seat. A couple of Uncles were sitting on the back tailgate with their feet hanging down.

"Christopher," I asked. "Is the Spider Tree on his road? Or do we have to drive off of the road to get to it?"

"It's on this road. It's up there," he said, pointing to some invisible place.

The truck moved along slowly for a while, and then Christopher shouted out, "Stop the truck." The truck came to an abrupt stop, jarring everyone as they reached out to keep from falling. I asked Christopher, "Did something happen to frighten you?"

He answered quietly, a little embarrassed, "We are getting real close to the Spider Tree."

"Do you want more help to protect you from the Spider Tree?" He nods his head sheepishly.

"Who do you want to call for help, to you get past the Spider Tree?" He was silent.

I realized he didn't know who to call. It wasn't enough. All of his family support system was already with him and he was still afraid. I could read in his face that he thought there was no one else to call.

"Is there someone special you want to call? Do you think we need to call in the police?"

His head lifted, eyes still shut tight, focused on his internal screen, aware of the danger that was just a ways up the road. I could imagine his surprise that Posie knew the police. Would they come for him?

"That's a good idea."

I told him to keep a lookout. The police would be coming in their squad cars. I told him I talked with the police chief, who remembered Posie and all the clowns from the parade. All the clowns who made everyone laugh and have a good time. The police chief said he was sending ten cars with officers who were trained to protect and keep everyone safe and free from danger, no matter what the danger was. The police department guarded the parade route every year and was glad to help a friend of the Clowns. Christopher relaxed as he waited and then I saw something register on his face.

I asked, "Do you see them coming?" He nodded with a small smile.

He said, "They have rifles and big nets to scoop up the spiders if they come too close to the truck."

"Great," I said. "Do you feel ready to start the truck and move on?" He nodded.

I said, "Okay! When everyone is in their place and you

are ready, give the driver instructions to start."

The truck resumed its course and rolled toward the Tree. There was no getting away from it. The road came very close to the Tree. The truck had to drive up close in order to pass the tree. Close enough that Christopher could easily reach out to touch the spiders. Creepy. The truck was moving along, the squad cars flanking both sides, front and back. Some of the police in their riot gear were holding on to the wooden panels as they hung from the sides of the truck, making sure none of the spiders blew into the truck or climbed up into the bed of the truck. I thought Christopher might make it this time. We were very close to the Tree when I saw him give way to his fear. He screamed. "Stop!"

The driver hit the brakes so instantaneously that everyone lurched forward. The police halted at the ready, waiting for instructions. What kind of fear is it that could devour a child like this? "Christopher," I managed. "I just heard from the Armed Forces. Police chief let them know what you were up against and he has alerted the Armed Forces. They are waiting to hear from you. Do you want them to come?"

His face shone with new hope. He hadn't run out of helpers. He hadn't run out of hope. The army guys wanted to come and help. They were waiting for his decision. They were waiting for Posie to call them. He thought for a moment, a bit relieved. He decided that the Army would be good. I reassured him that he made a wise choice. I urgently called, "Generals of the United States Army, my friend, Christopher needs your help and protection. He knows that you are very well trained to help when there is danger and that you stand ready to come and help him. Please come to meet him near the truck with the wooden panels on the back; the one that is close to the Spider Tree."

I turned to him and said, "Christopher, The United States Army is on its way. The Army that protects our entire country from harm. Protects us so that we don't have to live in fear. They are coming to protect you from your fear." I told him, "When you see them coming, I want you to tell the generals what you need.

Tell them where you want the army guys to stand. Okay?" A few moments of silence. Then, he said, " I see them coming."

I asked, "Are they marching, or are they arriving in big trucks or planes?" He looked carefully. "There are a lot of them marching. Some are jumping out of the trucks."

"I hear something. Christopher, look up. Do you see them jumping out of the planes with parachutes?" He raised this head.

His eyes were still shut tight, watching the movie screen in his head. He tilted his head back, facing into the bright life-giving sunshine. I heard his tiny voice in amazement say, "So many!"

I instructed, "As they arrive, they will need direction. You're in charge. Tell each group of soldiers where you want them to guard." He straightened, sitting taller in the large embracing chair. As the soldiers were pouring in, Christopher began to call out instructions. "I want some of you all around the truck near the police squad cars and some with me, up here, next to the boards."

"Christopher, can you see the soldiers? Are they doing exactly what you asked them to do? Do you feel safe with where they are positioned?"

"Yeah," he nodded.

I directed his attention to the front and the rear of the truck. "Do you see them? They are walking in front of the truck and some are guarding the back so that nothing can get past them." He nodded with his eyes still shut tightly, Yes, he could see them. I asked, "How do you feel now, when you see all of the policemen and soldiers who have come to help you?" His face had a relieved glow. He said he was okay.

I asked, "Are you feeling afraid?"

"No, I'm okay."

"When you are ready, ask the driver to start the truck again and to move slowly because there are so many soldiers and policemen around the truck." He agreed, and I heard him give directions to the driver to start moving out slowly. I reminded him, "If you begin to feel afraid, tell the driver to stop and we will get more help, okay?" He quickly nodded his head with new confidence this time.

The truck started moving. It was headed toward the Spider Tree. The Tree was huge. From far away it hadn't appeared so large. The trunk was like three trunks together. It was tall, piercing into the clouds. It blocked out the strong warm life-giving rays of the golden sun. Worst of all, it was covered with thousands of spiders of every shape, size, and color. Some larger than a big man's fist. We were coming alongside now. I watched Christopher's face grimace. Calmly, I checked in with him. "Is it time to stop?"

"No, we are too close," he said. Fear kept him from looking around. "Don't stop. Keep going." He's a brave child, holding on. When I saw him, white-knuckled, I suggested, "Tell the soldiers to keep the spiders away from the truck."

I heard him call out to the soldiers.

I asked, "Are they keeping the spiders away?"

"Yeah," he said.

"Are they using their nets to keep them away?"

"Yeah," he said. The truck was slowly passing the huge Spider Tree. We were all looking back to see it behind us. Everyone who came to help cheered and then they left waving to Christopher, sharing happy smiles, and calls of good luck. I waited till everything settled down.

"Christopher, look around. Where are you?"

"I don't know."

"Do you feel afraid?"

"No."

"Can you tell me what it looks like where you are?"

He said in his small voice with a new intensity, "It is

SOOO beautiful here. Everything is full of colors. It is very quiet."

I asked, "Are you alone? Are there other people with you?"

"There is someone here."

"Do you know who it is?"

"It's Jesus," he said simply.

For a moment, I was startled. This little boy was not a churchgoer. He came with his little friend from the church to talk to me. I was surprised to hear him speak the name of Jesus. I responded. "Is Jesus close to you?"

"Yeah, He's right here."

"Do you think He wants to talk to you?"

"Yeah, He's smiling at me."

"Okay," I said. " You go with Jesus and have a talk. Be sure to listen to everything he tells you, and ask all the questions you can think of. Okay?"

"Yeah," he said with a deep, knowing smile.

I left them in the quiet. I watched silently until I saw him stir. It was several minutes. I spoke softly. "Christopher, did you finish your talk with Jesus?"

"Yes," he said.

I asked, "Is Jesus still with you?"
"Yes."

"Is there anything else you want to ask Him before you come back? If not, take some time to say goodbye to him and thank him for talking to you. When you are all finished saying goodbye, take some deep breaths and come back to this room. I'll know you have come back when you open your eyes and look at me. Okay?"

"Okay."

It felt like a long time, that goodbye. He opened his eyes. I held my gaze gently on him, watching his eyes as he began to focus. He looked at me with a radiant, gentle smile. I waited, not wanting to rush him. When he was fully back and his consciousness returned to his body, I asked, "Christopher, would you like to tell me what happened?" He acknowledged my request with a simple nod of his head.

"You said it was very beautiful?"

"Yes. Lots of flowers and everything was nice."

"And you met Jesus. Did He talk to you?"

"Yes. He let me sit on His lap to talk."

"Would you like to tell me what you talked about? You don't have to if you don't want to."

I was aware that I had shifted away from asking questions to help Christopher's process. I was asking questions to quiet the yearning of my own desire to know. I felt that something profound, beyond my understanding, had just happened, and was still happening. I longed to understand this profound moment. Maybe it was beyond words. Christopher looked at me. I saw something new in his eyes. His young face softened by whatever was happening in the depths of his soul. In that moment, I saw a shift in his eyes; a deep wisdom that I didn't see before this.

He looked directly at me. Maybe he looked directly through me. The depth of his knowing and the intensity of his eyes made me weep. I couldn't stop the tears from flowing. He continued to gaze at me. I didn't want to be weeping in front of a "client", a young boy at that—a child. I had no choice. Tears simply streaked my face. He looked at them. I could feel his gaze.

I said, "I am not sad. I am crying tears of joy. You were afraid and now you aren't." That's all I could say to this child who transformed into a wise old sage, sitting in my office in the embrace of a large-winged chair, right before my eyes.

I didn't say that to him. I don't know if he would have understood. He might have. In that moment, I didn't know who I was talking to. So much about the nine-year-old vanished. What remained was a deeply grounded presence, rooted in the love of Christ, gazing at my tears with a love I could feel, an unspoken knowing.

That week, Christopher's mother phoned to thank me. She reported that after Christopher talked with me, the recurring nightmares ceased. The family was able to sleep, and all was peaceful.

I was grateful that she called. Often there is no follow-up, no report. I never hear the outcome. I thanked her. Told her I was glad I could help. If she needed to call again, don't hesitate. It was a week or so later, and his mother phoned again. I thought maybe he was experiencing a relapse. Perhaps there was more that needed to be done. Her voice was soft and measured. I could tell something wasn't quite right. I asked, "How is Christopher doing?" She said, "That's what I am calling about. He died peacefully in his sleep. I thought you would like to know." I heard her breath catch, a gentle sob. "He's gone!"

I felt a sword pierce my heart, just as it jumped with awareness and awe!

The dream was about his fear of death. He knew in his little boy way that he was dying. Cystic Fibrosis was taking his life.

Moving past the Spider Tree, past the terror, the fear, he stepped into another dimension; a place filled with love of Spirit and assurance that all was well. His calmness and the depth in his eyes, the knowing that it was all right to make the transition now. A loving Christ presence was waiting for him. He had a friend on the other side of there. There was nothing else he needed. He gave a week or two of peaceful nights to his family, a farewell gift.

He was free.

Once more that little boy with huge wisdom, the timeless wise old sage, made me cry.

Tears of Joy.

Tears of Wonder.

Tears of Awe.

Tears of deep knowing

That only come in gifted moments such as these.

Springbreak Independence

by Lin Bincle

It's the holiday season.

The time of travel and celebration.

You have made great progress

Preparing for your freedom and independence.

You are only bringing four bags this time!

I heave them into the waiting elevator, and inventory
your prep work.

One hardshell suitcase holds all the clothes you'll need

plus special "don't be homesick" bedding, including a
favorite pillow.

Your forest-themed, school backpack

conceals a Chromebook and

assignments that won't get done.

A simple see-thru toiletry sack

packed hurriedly before dashing out the door.

A cooler crammed full of liquid refreshments.

The soft vinyl sides bulge out in wonky directions.

A pink icebox, smothered with noxious green and yellow

polka dot plugs.

Threads split along a tattered top seam, fashioning a

gaping hole; the result of

Being overpacked, repacked, and toted for years.

Sand from a previous trip to the beach

has surely worked its way into the lining of the old cooler.

I silently slide my hand into

the crevice, searching for traces of grit. There is none.

The elevator door buzzes, then slides shut;

ending the respite reverie.

"Fifth floor, please," you tell the other passenger.

They nod, knowing that number means you are in for a
long stay.

I quiz you. "Exactly why do you plan to needle the nurse
for a travel size toothpaste?"

{ Lin Bincle, 2019, written from a window seat of UH
Rainbow Hospital, revised. }

The Teacher's Lesson

by Russell Henley

The Middle-East

Her husband plead for her to stay home. His colleague had been targeted the night before, and the fear that he and his wife might be next was evident in his voice.

"You know that any government worker is a special target. They know us all. He was not as high up either, and you know that the higher you are, the more likely you are to be targeted. Just read what's happening in the other cities."

He followed her around the small kitchen as she busily prepared her lunch to take with her. But, no matter how she turned in avoidance, he remained relentlessly behind her with his pleading. Finally, with her work finished, she turned, facing him to express herself.

"Yes, you work for the government, and yes—so did he. But I represent as much of us as you do. Those children in that car were not just any children, but unless you forgot, I taught them just last year. My teaching is...", dare she say it, "...it's just as important as your job."

He looked into her teary brown eyes in near disbelief.

He had never heard her stand up for herself as she was now,

never heard her speak with such conviction, never seen her so independent, independent of *him*. They stood still in front of each other.

"The children need me, they need their teacher," she quietly said. He insisted on taking her to the daycare in his car. There was no way he was going to let her ride the bus— not with their city now counted among the terrorized. She waited in the house while he started the car, just in case.

On the way, they drove past their friends' house. Mourners—possibly family—had arrived, and some were likely taking care of things. Neither one of them could imagine what there might be that needed cared for, though. The whole family was gone. Father. Mother. Son. Daughter. All dismembered and burned beyond recognition. She thought about what, if anything, she should tell her class. Even though they were preschoolers, there was no way the children wouldn't be affected by the attack.

The blast happened on the same street as the school, and when she called, she heard that there had been debris retrieved from the playground. She thought about what indoor activities she could have for the children that day.

As they arrived at the daycare, she saw that far down the street there was still a surprising amount of activity left over from the evening before. Everyone in the country had been told fear was the enemy and daily life must go on. But that didn't mean the neighborhood wasn't affected. Not too far away from the strained normalcy of the daycare, things were hugely different. Police with automatic weapons and riot gear stood guard around a blackened cordoned off area where the frame of the burnt car still lay where it had landed. Firemen worked at putting away the last of their gear. Anonymous people in white suits and holding black plastic bags were intently looking at the ground. Each stooped down every once in a while, picked up some little thing, and dropped it in the bag.

There was a news crew and half a dozen photographers pacing around the scene like scavengers around a carcass. Glass was being swept from under the gaping holes in walls where windows once were. Farther away from the epicenter, people seemed to be going about their usual daily business, except for occasionally changing direction to avoid the bomb site.

At the daycare, parents were escorting their children into the building rather than leaving them at the front doors and letting the staff take them in from there. Her husband leaned over to kiss her and gave her a long hug. That, too, was different. She had been assigned the class that was starting formal schooling in two weeks, and she was charged with teaching the children the first simple lessons that would prepare them. The classroom activity seemed pretty normal, the little ones coming in and dutifully putting their lunches and jackets away.

There was horseplay that needed to be stopped, and one child was sobbing quietly as she almost always did, having not quite adjusted to being there yet. As the children arrived, she mentally took attendance and noticed to her astonishment—and maybe even pride—that all of her children were indeed present. What a defiant statement her class was making.

"How is everyone, today?" She always asked that question. It was her way of getting their attention. But today, she genuinely wanted to know.

"We're good," they all said gathering around her in what mimicked a semi-circle on the floor.

"Mommy cried last night."

Looking at the little boy who had said it she asked, "Why did your mommy cry?"

"Because of the bomb," he said, rather matter-of-factly. *'Bomb' should not be in this boy's vocabulary.*

Before she could say anything, the other children took the chance to thrust their little arms in the air and ask their own questions.

"Where was it?"

"Do they only come at night?"

"What does it look like?"

"Did somebody shoot them with a tank?"

"What does it feel like?"

The questions were coming in rapid-fire succession, and each one seemed more intense and deeper than the one before; as if the children knew the subject was taboo or at least should be to them.

"Wait a minute, wait a minute," she said, holding up her hands, quieting the room. They all sat forward in anticipation, their collective inquisitive attitude making her more than nervous. Perhaps one of the aims of terrorism is making teachers like her explain true terror to young students.

"Let me explain the best I can. First, there's no reason to be afraid."

Great, she thought, *start out by lying to them*. She went on to explain that the "boom" was the only one that had ever happened in their city, and that the terrorists, who she called "the bad people", were only trying to scare certain people who they thought didn't like them. She could see in the innocent faces looking up to her that she was losing them to confusion as she tried to delicately explain car bombs. Not knowing what more to say, she finally just asked, "Do you understand?"

One little boy raised his hand, his shoulder tilted up to make his reach higher.

"Yes?", she asked.

"My brother said they were blown to little bits and that their heads were blown off."

She stared at the boy in disbelief as all the children looked at her as though there was nothing incongruous about his statement. Her heartbeat became audible in her head as she succumbed to the emotion that the one surreal statement brought. She felt rage at the boy's brother, rage at the terrorists for doing this to her class, rage at the broken school windows, rage at the blackened burnt debris, rage at her husband's concern, rage at her loss of words, rage at the tiny pieces of child flesh rotting in the sun outside her classroom.

She looked at the boy and felt his statement burrow deeper as it searched her soul for something she could say back to it.

"Yes," she finally said, "the people in the car were blown up," a fact grown in reality, but tempered by, "but they didn't feel it."

The heavy silence bore an even heavier truth that changed everything. She felt an odd peace in knowing that she had been honest with her class, and had started them as safely as she could on the path to the reality they would have to face for the rest of their lives. In their faces, she saw that she had—at least for now—satisfied some of their curiosity.

There was a gentle knock at the classroom door. A teacher from another class motioned her to the hallway.

"One of my girls fainted," the teacher explained, "and I need to take her home, but I'm afraid to go by myself. Would you go with us? We can get our classes together and have someone watch them. We won't be gone long."

The other teacher was obviously very distraught, and she felt she could not say no to her. The plans were, after all, already made.

"Alright, but let's get two assistants to watch our classes separately. I don't want to disturb the children more than necessary."

She put her arm on the younger teacher's shoulder to reassure her that everything was going to be alright. They would take the school van.

"Where's the teacher going?" the class asked their sitter.

"Well, another little girl in another class isn't feeling well, so that little girl's teacher and your teacher are going to take the little girl home. In fact, look out the window way over there." She pointed off into the distance past the school yard to the top of a van parked among other cars.

"Your teacher's going to drive the school van over here so the little girl doesn't have to walk out in the hot sun." The class stood up and turned around to peer through the classroom windows and search for their teacher. She closed the door of the van, turned the key in the ignition, and detonated the bomb. The muffled explosion lifted the van into the air and blew out the windows in front of the fire ball.

As a pink mist floated in the air outside a little girl broke the silence, "She didn't feel it, right?"

Unintended Gifts

by Hollie Petit

It was May 2001. I just completed my doctoral coursework and comprehensive exams. I still had to finish my dissertation, but I finally felt that my major life goals were within reach.

A couple of weeks prior, my grandmother was diagnosed with terminal cancer. We were close, and I wasn't prepared for life without her. She was so healthy; I thought she'd live forever. Some doors are hard to close—perhaps because they remind us that someday our doors will close, too. I was tired of thinking and feeling and doing. Needing to shut down the voices that said, "What's the point? We're all going to die," I challenged myself to think of what I wanted instead of what I didn't want. I closed my eyes and drifted into a restful state, where I let my mind wander.

Immediately, I thought about all the places I wanted to see in the world before the sands of time ran out on my life. My imagination took me on a journey around the world. At the time, I was a flight attendant with travel benefits and a week off from work. I wanted to go somewhere fun, but I didn't have any friends or family members available to travel. I wanted to be the wild and brave girl who took a trip to a new place all by herself, but I was afraid.

Fear gets in the way of most dreams. It's always there to remind us that what we want is too risky, costly, selfish, and absurd. It silences the voices that say, "You're going to regret not going for what you want." Fear usually wins.

My restless mind would not leave me alone. It tortured me into the night, even as I tried to distract myself by attending a concert with friends. They noticed I was a little off and asked me what was going on. I said, "I think I need to go to Italy tomorrow." They thought I was kidding. By the following day, I was burning with desire. I checked the flight loads to Italy, packed my bags, and called my mom on the way to the airport. I stopped at a bookstore along the way to get a book about Italy to know how to navigate when I arrived.

While standing in line to buy the book, I ran into a friend from ages past. He asked what I was doing. I said, "I think I'm going to Italy in a few hours." He said, "What do you mean *you think* you are going to Italy?" I explained that I just decided to go that morning and that I was hoping I could get on the flight if a seat were available." He looked at me like I was half crazy, but I sensed that he secretly wished that he could be so spontaneous and free.

There was no backing down now. I parked my vehicle, cleared security, and stood in line at the airport. Luckily, there was space available on the flight, so I was on my way to Italy—specifically, Rome. Once seated, I quickly dug into my book so that I was prepared once the plane landed.

My heart raced in excitement and terror as I prepared for my first solo international vacation. Sitting in the last window seat in the last row of the plane, I felt like I was meant to be there.

We landed. I purposefully marched out of the airport and onto public transportation to downtown Rome. Even though I hadn't slept in over a day, I hadn't felt this alive and vibrant in a long time. Exiting the train, I hit a sauna that reminded me that I was wearing way too many clothes. After visiting a dozen hotels, all of which were booked, I started to panic. Fortunately, someone recommended that I check the Madri Pie—a local monastery that housed guests in simple rooms at a minimal charge. My room overlooked the dome of St. Peter's Basilica. Tears flooded my eyes while taking in the splendor of the scenery, my journey, and all the events that flowed effortlessly to get me to that spot.

The following day, resident nuns served guests a simple breakfast of croissants with butter and jelly. I watched the graceful and devoted ladies do their daily tasks without hesitation or complaint. Having gone to Catholic schools for most of my life, I always felt admiration for and fear of these women. I tended to like the progressive ones who shirked off the customary habit over the old-school nuns who chose the traditional black and white garb—possibly because I was a bit of a rebel. I even wanted to be a nun in my younger years, but that was before I faced various existential crises that encouraged me to choose a spiritual path that was more fitting for me. Sitting at the dining table, lost in memories, I found myself soul searching.

There are moments in life that define us—times when we fall and times when we rise to the challenge. These are turning points in how we see ourselves and what defines us as individuals. Traveling to Rome was one of those times for me. I didn't make the trip to prove anything to others; instead, I wanted to prove it to myself. More importantly, I gained a tremendous sense of freedom that I will never forget—a type of freedom that I had never known.

From the time I got up until the time I went to bed, I was on my own. I explored, ate, lingered, and observed whatever I wanted for as long as I wanted. I wrote a lot and took many pictures to capture the times I witnessed beauty or gained insights about life. It's incredible what the mind can comprehend when it is in a new environment without its everyday restrictions. Everything felt revelatory.

Sure, I did the touristy things—visited the Vatican, St. Peter's Basilica, and the Colosseum, among other locations. I savored gelato on the Spanish Steps, bought my grandmother a rosary, and lingered over religious art. But what happened around me paled in comparison to what happened within me. The experiences I had were transcendent. While all the scenery and food were divine, what changed me was stepping out of my usual ways of being —the routine, expectations, and norms of everyday life.

With all that stripped away, I made space for a different type of intentionality. It was in that space, one in which I got to choose how to engage each moment, that I became aware of what I wanted and what I didn't want. Moments like these invite us to imagine our lives anew.

Moments like these can change the trajectory of our lives.

While in Rome, I made a lot of decisions. The time away from my daily life gave me a perspective to evaluate my life. I vowed to spend more time with my grandmother and learn more about her life while still alive. I planned on moving to Colorado when my grandmother had passed. I committed myself to being open to love for the first time in over a decade. I remained steadfast in my goals of finishing my degree and becoming a professor. Not surprisingly, all those things came to fruition.

Sometimes, a little distance is needed from our lives to be able to see it clearly. Too often, we get caught up in the rat race, and we can't see the forest through the trees. Nowadays, I can't always jet off to a foreign country because I am caring for aging family members. Still, I find ways to get into new spaces—a walk in the woods, a long drive, and challenging myself to a new experience or adventure. Such an exercise must be done mindfully, though, to maximize the experience. If we don't contemplate where we have been and where we are going, our days may pass us up and we might never do what we really want.

In my grandmother's final days, she was surrounded by many children, grandchildren, and friends. She made it to the age of 84, which she spent healthily until the end. She lived a high-quality life according to most standards. Still, I wonder if her life was all that she wished it would be. I hope that I dare to live deliberately until my final days. And to the one who scatters my ashes on the breeze, I hope he or she is reminded that life is finite and should be lived intentionally and joyfully.

The Yellow Rose

by Don Truex

Like the yellow rose is my love for you.

True in its richness of color, profound in its opulence of beauty.

The luxury it shares is for all to see,

So my love showers you.

Splendor in the sun cannot be denied. Only joined in our

lives of togetherness.

Lavishness grooms your every being, softness dims not. loneliness is not allowed.

Fullness finds a new birth as my lips of color slide over... caressing your forehead, cheeks and lips.

So my love showers you.

Commitment, yes true love rules with unconditional, absolute daring affection.

Vibrancy meant for animation only the heart can summon and understand.

Resonance like the master's violin; relished, adored by the ears of the heart.

So my love showers you.

There is no unconsciousness of poverty, no scarcity in the color of the yellow rose, nor in my love for you.

Unfathomable is the heart, mysterious are its ways.

Hidden meaning it has not.

So my love showers you.

2 0 2 0

by Lin Bincle

C   an't be your lover

O   pen to friendship

V   ixen anguished-I am not

I   ndecisive nation of chaos

D   on't die

Lin Bincle, 2020,

Originally a text message with emojis too.

Author Bios

Alison McBain

Alison McBain is an award-winning author with poems & stories published in Litro, Write City Magazine, and Yellow Arrow Journal. When not writing, she is an editor for the monthly literary magazine Scribes *MICRO* Fiction (fairfieldscribes.com). In her free time, she pens the comic Toddler Times, does origami meditation, and draws all over the walls of her house with the enthusiastic help of her kids. More at: alisonmcbain.com.

Ben Bisbee

A dreamer, a doer, a madman with focus, Ben Bisbee considers himself the good kind of dangerous. Working during the day as a nonprofit engagement and development expert, Ben moonlights as a content creator, producer, and fiction and non-fiction writer of various creative, community, and chaotic topics. Ben is a published author and currently the host and creator of AQUEERD, an web-based interview show and clothing line on a mission to hand the microphone to queer people who are loud, proud, and choose to embrace their aqueerdness each and every day. He lives in Northeast Ohio with his husband, Joe, and their 11 cats.

Ben DiCola

Ben DiCola is a freelance sports writer who played second base in his prime. While he couldn't hit much, Ben was adept in the field and could steal a base or two. His writing career has lasted much longer, having covered numerous high school and college football, basketball and baseball games spanning over 40 years, as well as broadcasting such events in Stark County.

Brett A. Tipton

Brett A. Tipton currently teaches online English classes to kids in China. He's studying digital video media technology at Stark State College. He enjoys writing, playing his ukulele, and music creation. In the past he's taught a wide variety of speech, writing, management, and math classes at the college level. He enjoys writing on a wide variety of topics and various genres.

Dr. Carol P. Vaccariello, D. Min., LPC, Pilgrim

Carol is writing a SEED collection of stories on different aspects of her life experience. Each SEED Chapter will germinate a book of similar stories. Carol's writing is based on life experience, some are incredible, for example, the year before Covid she traveled to a Monastery in Spain during April with plans to return home in May. Carol was spirit-led, returning home after a five-month unplanned journey. This unexpected pilgrimage is a riveting story, filled with radical trust, a fractured foot and past life love. During her most recent Walk across Spain, she recorded plant songs as she walked. Some of these songs are unlike any she has recorded to date. She is a plant whisperer, collecting Plant songs wherever she travels. Carol shares with groups who are eager to experience plants singing, to hear their own plants sing. Highly intuitive and a natural healer, she has honed her skills as a Medical Intuitive, Energy and Distance Healer.

Called upon by medical professionals when modern technology fails. To stay healthy, she inspires others as a certificated Silver Sneakers Instructor, leading classes in Yoga Stretch, Classic Aerobics, Water Aerobics, Tai Chi/Qi Gong, Meditation and Stress Management. Carol is a Spiritual Life Coach, Storyteller, Public Speaker. Leads Workshops/Seminars. She is a life-long learner of Consciousness Evolution, Astral Travel, Dream Work, Mysticism and much more. Doctor Vaccariello is currently accepting Life coaching clients.

*Author: The Lion of God: Archangel Ari'El ...personal encounters.

*Contributing Author: Order of Sacred Earth, A Strange Vocation, Writers' Anthology 2018, Writers' Anthology 2019, Writers' Anthology 2020, Writers' Anthology 2021

*Online interviews: YouTube, enter: Carol Vaccariello

*Contact: Facebook/Carol Vaccariello,

snowswan12@gmail.com, www.windsofspirit.net

Diane L. Johnson

Diane L. Johnson is an native of Akron, Ohio. She is a writer and visual artist. Her passion for writing fiction, devotions and poetry is synonymous with her love for painting. She is co-founder of Art Only Boutique, LLC. and co-founder of ABAG (Akron Black Artist Guild). Diane has taught several creative classes in writing and mixed media. She is a retired secretary from the public-school district. Mother of two adult children and eight beautiful grandchildren.

Hollie Petit

Hollie Petit, Ph.D., is an author of nonfiction books and articles that focus on spirituality, creativity, travel, health, happiness, and humor. She traveled the world searching for life experiences and stories, which are the foundation of many of her writings. Hollie considers creativity to be the most significant source of motivation available to all living beings. When not writing, she enjoys spending time with her husband and many rescued dogs and cats. https://www.holliepetit.com/

James Valentino

Freelance writer, and blogger (MAD MAN ON A GREAT LAKE), James Valentino has been a member of the Akron Writer's Group for the past few years. His short story, A Night at the Concert, was published in 2019's anthology and two more were included in last year's publication. Up until the current pandemic, has made the effort to attend the group's meetings in Akron on a regular basis. Besides a few pieces in the local newspapers up in Cleveland, James (or Jim as his friends know him) has written a few (unproduced) screenplays over the years and some non-fiction. A Cleveland native, Jim has a Bachelor's Degree in Arts and Science (Creative Writing) from Cleveland State University, a Masters Degree in Urban Planning, Design, and Development from the Maxine Goodman Levin College of Urban Affairs at Cleveland State and a certified technical writer. He is currently a case management clerk at the Court of Appeals, Juvenile Division, of Cuyahoga County where, among other things, the editor/publisher of the department newsletter, Clerk's Corner.

Joanne Kilgour Dowdy

Dr. Dowdy completed her Ph.D. in Literacy Studies at the University of North Carolina in Chapel Hill. She combines her education in literacy with her theater degree from Juilliard to help teachers become more effective in the classroom. Dr. Dowdy's primary research interests include documenting the experiences of Black women involved in education from adult basic literacy to higher education. She has published 16 books and her children's book about her father has been translated into Haitian Kreyòl.

Jodie West

Jodie West has a degree in English Literature from Claremont McKenna College. She is an elementary school science teacher and was featured as one of 50 subjects in the documentary *Go Public; A Day in the Life of an American School District*. Jodie has been published on theravensperch.com, as well as in the literary journal, *Humana Obscura*. She lives in California with her family.

Ken Rogers

In addition to writing short fiction, Ken Rogers works as a blogger, journalist, technical writer, and teacher in northeast Ohio. While writing and reading are his favorite activities, he's also fond of doing his own yard work, which he does reasonably well, and grilling, where his success has been decidedly intermittent.

Kora Sadler

I have been in the writing industry since 2014 as the founder and member of the writing community, The Writers Group. My strong leadership skills and diverse background gives me a unique insight into how writers & authors can live their dreams through the power of storytelling; and since 2018 I decided to pursue a career (by divine intervention) into the publishing industry full-time. As a creative individual I understand what it takes for others to become successful and my passion for helping people find success is what drives me everyday. It doesn't matter if you're looking for advice on how to start writing, self-publishing, or marketing your book; I will be there with you every step of the way. In addition to being a writer myself, I am an expert in the fields of holistic health, healing, and nutrition. I write about spirituality, personal growth, and self-development. My goal is to help others become healthier versions of themselves by sharing my knowledge and education on holistic self-care practices with my own personal experience dealing with arthritis pain, dieting, and weight loss.

*Check Me Out: www.linktr.ee/korasadler

*Follow Me: @KoraSadler

*Tag Me: #KoraSadler

*Write With Me: #5PmWritersClub #5AmWritersClub

Lin Bincle

Lin Bincle is a Buckeye Born, nationally-oriented, reflective poet, author, and degreed futurist. In addition to the womb-to-tomb (life and death) selection in this anthology, she has assembled other writings; pondering topics of love, landscapes, values, longing, purpose, time-travel, health matters, science education, and more. She is a Rustbelt Migrant who recently returned to her northeast Ohio roots, where she enjoys fossil-hunting, spring flowers, autumn colors, scents, and all the sensations of a robust life. In total, her collection of creative works spans four decades, revealing the evolving perspective of a statistically Average American, navigating a tumultuous transition into the 21st century. Holding a Master's degree in *Studies of the Future*, from the University of Houston-Clear Lake (2000), she excels at generating clarity amid chaos. She is a person of ever-growing faith, inviting hope. Direct inquiries on her research, writing, and speaking engagements to ATTN: Bincle, linbrown@ymail.com

Louise Francis

I am Louise Francis, 46 year old divorced mother of three. I spent 24 years working in Social Services. Being locked in during Covid presented me with an opportunity to focus on my first true love... writing. I have loved writing poetry since elementary and have dabbled a little in short stories. I enjoy writing that shoots spunk, frankness and emotion. I would love to one day have a book of poetry as well as a book of short stories published one day.

Matthew Davenport

Matthew is a copywriter by day and a fiction writer and copy editor by night. He's a father to two sons, Isaak and Ben, and began his writing career at age 13. With a novella already published on Amazon, several edited anthologies under his belt, and a passion for written language, Matthew's aspirations reach far into the writing world and beyond. He hopes to finish his first novel soon and begin building a fan base.

Mindy Altrid

As you know, I'm a writer, but also an artist and a retired physician. The fictional stories I have written have sprung from my time treating patients as well as from my philosophical and creative spirit. Regarding my past history; I grew up in a city of near thirty-five thousand in the north-central part of Illinois. My higher education was at Loyola University of Chicago, followed by medical school at Loyola-Stritch School of Medicine. I treated patients for 25 years in Illinois before moving to Ohio where I continued to treat patients through 2016. Besides writing and painting, my time is filled with taking care of my home, gardening, hiking, some volunteering, and simply enjoying the fresh outdoor air and the beautiful plants and animals that nature provides. I wish you always, HAPPY TRAILS and GRIPPING TALES!

Nancy Rudisill

Nancy Rudisill is fifty-three years old. She lives in Cleveland, Ohio. She lives with her husband Glenn and son Johnny. She also has one very spoiled cat named Cocoa. She works full time as a LPN nurse, but has always found a way to and pursue her writing aspirations in her spare time. She has published one book, Through the Fire, and is currently working on a second book. She is very grateful to have found the Writer's Group and the support she has found within the group.

Russell Henley

Russell Henley enjoys writing flash fiction. His stories follow the same format he has used for almost forty years. He's accidentally adopted certain rules. His characters have no names, and death is always lurking among just a few words. When he's not writing or enjoying the company of his friends in The Writers Group, he is sharing a very happy life with his wife Angelica in their home in Akron, Ohio.

Steven Pryce

Steven Pryce graduated from Hillsdale College, winning the Ambler Literary Award. He then wrote articles for Sun Newspapers in Wadsworth and The Sun Journal in North Canton before independently publishing his fiction. He recently has been published in The Blue Collar Review, the Neighborhood Voices Anthology in Cleveland, and the Take Five Anthology. His writing has appeared in the Akron Beacon Journal and Treatment Advocacy Center's News and Features. He is also involved with NAMI Stark County and contributes to their newsletter. Tom Walker of Athens NAMI interviewed him for an NPR radio segment.

Community Support & Sponsors

"Do not say harmful things, but say what people need; words that will help others become stronger."
-Ephesians 4:29

Your purchase of The Writers Group Anthologies help provide resources, workshops, ongoing support, and encouragement for local writers of all levels and genres in pursuing their dreams of becoming published.

We offer positive feedback and methods that will ensure a new writer's first steps into writing are positive ones. For the more experienced writers we offer substantive critiques to help sharpen your work on its way to submission for publication.

We have many writers who have professional credits to their name in poetry, short stories or full-length novels. But whether you are just starting out or are an experienced writer with representation,The Writers Group can offer you guidance to reaching your goals.

For more information on joining The Writers Group or becoming a Sponsor, please visit

thewritersgroup.org

meetup.com/thewritersgroup

Or email us at: thewritersgrouporg@gmail.com

Made in the USA
Middletown, DE
30 September 2021

48717977R00179